MIND SET WIN

Red Bull

Exploring the mental recipes of high performers and how we can apply them ourselves

BENVENTO

INTRO

APPLYING THE EXTRA-ORDINARY TO THE EVERYDAY

Welcome to *Mind Set Win,* a book that has been developed out of the podcast of the same name from Red Bull – and is all about taking the kinds of mental techniques used by world-class athletes and other high performers and applying similar strategies to everyday life.

Over the following pages, you'll hear from many of the guests who've appeared on the podcast since its launch – and from others who have provided new interviews especially for the book.

Those featured include serial champions like Max Verstappen, Armand 'Mondo' Duplantis, Carissa Moore, and Marc Márquez, inspirational national team captains and World Cup winners Ben Stokes and Siya Kolisi, and boundary-pushing endurance athletes like Fernanda Maciel and Lucy Charles-Barclay – not to mention true icons of their respective sports like Lindsey Vonn and Daniel Dhers.

Then there are the behind-the-scenes operators – the team masterminds like Sébastien Debs, better known simply as Ceb in the world of gaming, and a number of practising sports psychologists.

They are joined within these pages by some of the world's most in-demand coaches, people like basketball's Chris Matthews, aka Lethal Shooter, and tennis players like Elena Rybakina and Matteo Berrettini, alongside stars of BMX and mountain biking, surfing, and skating, as well as the Olympic gold medal-winning breaker Phil Wizard.

The common thread between them is their shared commitment to excellence, as well as an understanding that mastering the mental side of their sport has been a vital part of their rise to the top.

Our goal in making the podcast was not only to hear these high performers giving first-hand insight into how they prepare mentally for elite competition, but also to go a stage further by showing how the rest of us can learn from their experience and put into practice the skills these athletes have worked on during their careers.

Can all these techniques be mastered by non-professionals? Well, perhaps not! Athletes dedicate a significant proportion of their training time, often over decades, to their mental performance.

However, in working with a number of high-performance psychologists – including the Head of Mental Performance at Red Bull's Athlete Performance Center, York-Peter Klöppel, and the show's presenters over three seasons, Cédric Dumont, Kate Courtney, and Lisa Ramuschkat – we've tried to break down what the guests have told us and provide a series of actionable insights and exercises that are related to the kind of work the psychological pros do, but which should be accessible to us all.

The book is structured in such a way that you can dive in and out of chapters, depending on your specific interest in the overarching theme or, of course, the stories of the athletes themselves.

Along the way, you'll hear some of the most inspiring people from the world of sport speaking candidly about subjects that align clearly with the development of a winning mindset – like facing fears (Chapter 3), finding flow state (Chapter 4), and keeping control (Chapter 11).

But as the stories of these outstanding characters make clear, the journey to being successful, and staying successful, can't just be a relentless crusade to be better, stronger, and more competitive. These people understand that developing a winning mindset is also about taking care of yourself, accepting that everyone makes mistakes, and avoiding falling into the trap of punishing yourself for setbacks that are, after all, inevitable.

That's why we've made a point of including chapters that are about being good to yourself (Chapter 6), accepting mistakes (Chapter 8), and coping with crisis (Chapter 9).

It's also important to highlight the two chapters that begin and end the book.

Finding ways to love what you do (Chapter 1), to savour the moment, to make choices based on what you enjoy doing and not just about what you think will bring you the most reward, is so important. If you want to be successful at something for a long time, there is no alternative but to have true passion.

The question of purpose (Chapter 12) comes up time and again with our guests on *Mind Set Win* too. They know that the tangible rewards that come with glory, though important, can never be enough by themselves, and that true fulfilment is the result of being motivated by a greater cause.

By building on the podcast and presenting *Mind Set Win* in book form, our aim is to elaborate even further upon, and connect the dots between, the different mental techniques we've featured on the show – and to bring you some new ones. Each of the 12 chapters will take you on a journey through a particular theme or mindset strategy, with steps you can apply in your own life.

Whether you're looking to enhance your performance at work, improve your mental resilience, achieve personal goals, or just feel more fulfilled and satisfied in general, we hope these insights will inspire and equip you to unlock your full potential.

So lean in and spend some quality time learning how these elite athletes have found an extra gear when they've really needed it, while maintaining the kind of balance that leads to long and sustained success.

A NOTE OF THANKS:

Many people have been involved in the making of *Mind Set Win,* and we couldn't have done it without them. The hosts of the first season were both world-class athletes in their own right – Cédric Dumont, the skydiver who is himself a high-performance psychologist, and Kate Courtney, a world champion star of downhill mountain biking. Their insights were vital in making good on the show's promise to break down the tactics used by professional athletes and make them not only understandable but also useful for anyone who is eager for self-improvement. Off mic, the psychologist Mia Stellberg provided crucial insights, based on her work with esports teams at the highest levels of international competition. York-Peter Klöppel, Head of Mental Performance at Red Bull's Athlete Performance Center, also offered psychological expertise from early on, and in season 2 he took on co-presenting duties with Cédric, helping to make the takeaways and exercises even more accessible for the audience. York continued in the studio for season 3, this time joined by Lisa Ramuschkat. Together, they added more substance to the episodes, with Lisa leading each guest in an in-depth interview before joining York for the breakdown.

Many more outstanding professionals have worked behind the scenes on the podcast in areas including research, editorial, and production, and in the writing, editing, design, and production of this book.

Heartfelt thanks go to you all, and especially to the athletes, coaches, managers, and psychologists who gave up their time, and spoke with such refreshing candour, offering the kind of insight the rest of us don't have – but can certainly learn from.

The Mind Set Win team

A note on the interviews:
All the interviews – whether recorded for the podcast or for the book – have been lightly edited for clarity, and shortened in order to highlight the techniques and experiences relevant to the chapter theme.

GUEST LIST

Q&A

YORK-PETER KLÖPPEL

As Head of Mental Performance at the Red Bull Athlete Performance Center, York-Peter Klöppel is part of a team dedicated to helping some of the world's best and most creative individuals prepare to reach peak performance when it really matters.

The APC, based in the Salzburg region of Austria, acts as an athlete accelerator, with a team of experts that includes nutritionists, physiotherapists, medical doctors, sport scientists, strength and conditioning coaches, and, of course, mental performance experts.

York will be a familiar voice to fans of the podcast *Mind Set Win*. He became a co-presenter in seasons 2 and 3, after initially offering his expertise behind the scenes. Before you dive in to the chapters, here he is explaining a little more about his role and what he hopes everybody will take away from this book.

What does your role as the Head of Mental Performance entail?

At the APC, we help athletes unlock their true potential and reach the next level. We have experts from every area of sports medicine and sports science, and I have the honour of leading the mental performance department. Alongside my team, I work with the athletes regularly to help them train their mental skills and find ways to perform when it really matters. It's a fun job and I get to meet a lot of interesting people.

How do you approach working with athletes across a wide variety of sports?

It's very important to treat everyone uniquely, as individuals. We listen to their individual needs and try to help them with what they perceive to be the most important aspects. We don't follow a specific programme or scheme, as not all motor-sport athletes are the same, for example. But having said that, people always think there's a big difference between all the sports, and while this might be true physically, from a mental perspective it's not always the case. Personalities differ but the challenges can be similar.

What is the importance of mental strength in high performance?

There are so many aspects of mental performance, many of which are included in this book. In an athletic sense, the importance of mental strength really becomes obvious during competition. You can put in hours and hours of work in training, but you still need to turn up on the day and reach your maximum potential if you want to succeed. And the difference between performing and not performing is often down to mental strength.

It's not just purely performance related, though. Other topics we explore in *Mind Set Win* include how to take better care of ourselves and why taking the time to look after ourselves is so important to being healthier in general.

THE DIFFERENCE BETWEEN PERFORMING AND NOT PERFORMING IS OFTEN DOWN TO MENTAL STRENGTH.

What will we learn from featuring the athletes all together in this book?

I think it's really important for people to know that the athletes don't see themselves as special. They're normal people like you or me, but what they do have is a relentless commitment and dedication to improve, the internal drive to not only achieve their goals but to become the best version of themselves.

At the end of their careers, they want to say they did everything they possibly could to reach their potential – and I hope that's the inspiration people take from *Mind Set Win*. People shouldn't think they're going to instantly become a world champion or record-holder, but rather discover how they too can become the best version of themselves.

How transferable to daily life are the mental tactics adopted by high-performance athletes?

They're very transferable, and we've explored this throughout *Mind Set Win* with the exercises that everybody can take away and action. I'm an example of this myself. I've also learned so much from the athletes that I incorporate into my daily life. Things like journaling and mindfulness practices have become very important for me, and I'm sure they can be for other people as well.

How has the approach to mental training changed over recent times?

There's been such a positive shift in perception. In the past, the traditional way of looking at psychology was to wait until something goes wrong before starting to look for an answer or skill that can help you with it. But a psychologist is more than just an option when everything else has failed and you have nobody else to turn to.

Nowadays, the mindset has changed in that mental training is being treated more like coaching. It's about improving your current wellbeing even if you feel great. And you don't have to wait for a problem to arise before doing it! You can realise benefits by starting to develop your mental strength, not just as a prevention strategy, but in order to see improvements in your life. Even when everything in your life is going well, you can still get so much out of continually developing your mental fitness, or seeing your psychologist, because it will help you consistently perform better. That's the mind shift that I've really strived for.

HAVING THE GOAL OF IMPROVING YOUR GENERAL WELLBEING AND SATISFACTION IS A GREAT PLACE TO START.

For people starting out on their mental fitness journey, what advice would you give?

It's good to remember that it's a process. There's nothing written in any book that you can read that will suddenly make everything seem better. It requires time and effort.

Also, having the goal of improving your general wellbeing and satisfaction is a great place to start. Try to develop a mindset that involves a continuous drive to self-improve and to be the best you can possibly be.

Each chapter ends with an actionable exercise. How should people approach these?

Not all the chapters will apply to everyone, so I wouldn't recommend starting with every exercise all at once. Pick out a couple and really commit to them before evaluating the results. I hope that some of the topics will stand out to you, and you'll have moments where you go, "Aha, that's what I've been looking for!"

CHAPTER 1

LOVING WHAT YOU DO

INTRODUCTION

HAVE YOU EVER NOTICED JUST HOW MUCH EASIER IT IS TO COMPLETE A CHALLENGING TASK WHEN YOU CAN APPROACH IT IN A POSITIVE FRAME OF MIND AND HAVE SOME FUN ALONG THE WAY?

IN THIS CHAPTER WE'LL LOOK AT:

Choosing your own path

Finding joy

Activating the senses

WE'LL HEAR FROM:

Jamie O'Brien
"It brought me so much joy, so much happiness and fun to film and create and build content and have them believe in what I believe in."

Lucy Charles-Barclay
"My performances got better as I took the pressure off and found that love again. My mental toughness and resilience went up another notch."

Justine Dupont
"I really enjoy this moment when riding a wave, and at the end I have a giant smile on my face as I know that I did all the right things at the right time."

Developing the ability to find satisfaction in the experience as well as in the results can help bring long-term success – something we've heard consistently on *Mind Set Win* from athletes, coaches, and other high performers.

They explain that enjoyment doesn't always need to be found in the winning moment or the crowning achievement. Sure, the results are important, as we're all striving to be more successful, but separating the outcome from the action and allowing ourselves to live in the moment is also at the core of increased productivity and ongoing success.

Whether it's Jamie O'Brien letting go of a key aspect of surfing to concentrate on what truly motivates him, Lucy Charles-Barclay finding herself smiling as she comes out of a punishing swim, or Justine Dupont activating her senses to live every moment of riding a big wave – it's their obvious enjoyment and passion that enables them to be the best version of themselves.

Of course, finding joy is a very personal thing and you can't just decide to be happy, but by learning to be present we can give ourselves the best opportunity to enjoy what we do on a daily basis. Let's learn how some of the very best go about it.

Red Bull
S3, EP 8
LISTEN TO THE
PODCAST HERE:

JAMIE O'BRIEN

GROWING UP ON THE NORTH SHORE, HAWAII, NEAR ONE OF THE MOST NOTORIOUS WAVES ON THE PLANET AND HAVING A LIFEGUARD DAD WITH A SURFING PASSION, MEANT JAMIE O'BRIEN WAS DESTINED FOR A LIFE ON THE WATER.

By 21, he was one of the youngest surfers ever to win a Pipeline Masters, generating excitement for his creativity and audacity in the water.

So it was totally unexpected when he turned his back on competition to travel the world and become a content creator. Three thrilling surf movies and his own surf school later, Jamie dropped in to *Mind Set Win* to talk about the importance of staying true to what you love.

" —

I beat all my heroes when I was 21 years old. I'm going, "Wait, what just happened? This is astronomical." And then all the sponsors started looking at me. And for me, it was like, "That feels good to win but I don't really want to continue competing." Because I wasn't even at the highest level; I was a level below still. And I felt like it was a lot of pressure from the sponsors.

I was watching all these videos of free surfers, and I just really liked that realm of filming and creating and building content. At that time, I was already doing that with my friends – we would travel the world, and we'd take turns filming each other, and to me, that was so cool. Then I started realising I wanted to make a movie, and so this was the turning point, from surfing contests to making videos.

I remember saying, "Dad, I want to make a movie!" But my dad wanted me to be world champion. He was pissed because I saw a different vision than the way he saw me going.

I just remember talking to a sponsor and saying, "We want to make a Jamie O'Brien movie." And you know what they told me? "We are not ready

for a Jamie O'Brien movie." So I decided I was going to make it with or without them. We showed it to them before we released it and they said, "Wow, this is beautiful – we would love to be a part of it!"

It brought me so much joy, so much happiness and fun to film and create and build content and have them believe in what I believe in. And it just opened the floodgates. We're like, "Oh my God, we love filming; this is epic!" You want to do what you love.

And Jamie's ambitions didn't stop at filmmaking; he also founded his own surf school on the North Shore of Hawaii...

I always wanted to open up a surf school. I liked the idea of teaching people how to surf and giving the gift of surfing to the world, because that's what my father did for me, and it changed my life. It wasn't easy but you've got to set your goals so high and think, "I'm going to achieve them one day." Now we teach thousands and thousands of people how to surf every year, and it's such a beautiful thing. It reminds me why I love surfing.

I'd like my legacy to be giving the gift of surfing to everybody, but then also giving the choice of what you do. Just know, there's not one right way to ride a surfboard or to film and create content. Be yourself, be unique, and do it how you want to do it. And that's how you will succeed – by being yourself.

YORK'S NOTES

If you're skilled at something, and especially if you've started to achieve some success at it, it can be all too easy to get swept along without stopping to consider whether it makes you happy and fulfilled. In the midst of huge success, Jamie braved his dad's disappointment and decided to dedicate himself to what truly brought him satisfaction. It must have taken a lot of self-awareness and courage for him to admit that his passion was becoming a pressure. But here's the cool thing: by doing something that was his own idea and something he felt he had a lot of autonomy over (the movie), he was able to reconnect with what gave him joy and use it to guide him forward. As we progress with our goals, it's so important to keep checking in on how we feel. Because finding what makes you happy might not necessarily mean wholesale change. Instead, like Jamie, it might mean just a shift in emphasis and focus.

LUCY CHARLES-BARCLAY

THE BRITISH ATHLETE SWITCHED FROM SWIMMING TO TRIATHLON AND WON THE IRONMAN WORLD CHAMPIONSHIPS IN 2023 IN A NEW COURSE RECORD TIME.

Key to Lucy's rapid rise from rookie to champion in the punishing discipline combining swimming, cycling, and running has been the ability to find and maintain enjoyment in every part of the process. Preparing to race intensely against your rivals for more than eight hours requires unwavering levels of motivation, and Lucy has discovered how to find her mojo when she really needs it. Let's learn how she's able to smile through the pain.

“ —

When I first transitioned from swimming to IRONMAN, I enjoyed it because it was new. Everything was different and it felt exciting. Going out for a group ride at the weekend didn't even feel like training because you were talking and riding. It was so completely different to swimming, which always felt like a chore. I always found open water swimming more fun than swimming laps in the pool, though, as swimming outdoors felt like a hobby, something I enjoyed doing but was still getting a lot from.

To begin with, my swim was so useful in allowing me to get good results, even if my bike and run wasn't as strong as the other girls', as I could build up such a big lead. It convinced me that I needed to start loving it again, as, actually, it's a weapon for me and sets every race up with a great start.

I was doing double days in the pool, morning and evening, and I remember ploughing up and down the pool and hitting times I wasn't hitting before. I would finish the sets absolutely in bits, but I'd be lying on the pool side with a massive smile on my face. I remembered that pushing myself and finding a new gear was what I loved about swimming. That was what really ignited the love again.

When I finished my first IRONMAN, I had never felt anything like it. In that moment, I knew that I had to keep doing it. Some training sessions are really tough and it's hard to have fun in that exact moment but after I've achieved it, I'm really happy and get a lot from it.

— ”

After many successful years as a professional, an extended break from competition allowed Lucy to remember why she finds so much joy in IRONMAN racing. This realisation, together with a new outlook, ignited a run of form that resulted in her becoming 70.3 world champion in 2021.

“ —

In hindsight, the year out with the pandemic was a blessing for me, as it allowed me to come away from the sport and reevaluate why I was doing it. It gave me so much energy and made me realise that I do love what I'm doing.

Then, in 2021, I probably had the best year of my career as a triathlete because I was like, "What does it matter what the outcome is? Just go enjoy it, have fun, and challenge myself in new ways." I wanted to do well, but if it went terribly, what does it even matter?

> MY PERFORMANCES GOT BETTER AS I TOOK THE PRESSURE OFF AND FOUND THAT LOVE AGAIN.

S1, EP 1

LISTEN TO THE PODCAST HERE:

My performances got better as I took the pressure off and found that love again. My mental toughness and resilience went up another notch.

There is a photo that was captured of me coming out of the swim at a race, and I just have pure joy on my face. It showed me that I just love it and that's why I do it. I can push myself to the limit and still be having fun at the same time.

What's that famous saying? If you do what you love, you'll never work a day in your life? That sounds bang on the mark for Lucy, who makes a point of finding fun in her training and day-to-day life, even as she puts in tremendous effort to be at her best. It helps her stay motivated and, along with all the training, is a vital ingredient in her success. She also has an ability to focus on the challenge in front of her, and the enjoyment of just being there. It's no surprise that developing this approach coincided with the best season of her career. Another part of her journey that's relatable is the realisation that taking a break from something you dedicate a lot of time to can often really spark that enjoyment again.

> *EVERY TIME I SURF A BIG WAVE, IT FEELS LIKE THE FIRST TIME I WENT SURFING WHEN I WAS YOUNGER. I'M ENJOYING EVERY SECOND!*

S1, EP 5

LISTEN TO THE PODCAST HERE:

JUSTINE DUPONT

WIDELY REGARDED AS ONE OF THE BEST BIG WAVE SURFERS OF HER GENERATION, VIDEOS OF JUSTINE RIDING JAW-DROPPING 70-FOOT WAVES HAVE BEEN VIEWED MILLIONS OF TIMES.

A world champion in multiple disciplines on the water, Justine has dedicated her career to chasing the biggest thrills that surf breaks such as Jaws in Hawaii and Nazaré in Portugal have to offer.

Performing in the eye of a storm isn't for the faint-hearted but through connecting with her senses and living in the present moment, the French surfer is able to come alive and enjoy every aspect of the experience.

" —

I love the ocean, big waves, and spending time in the water. Every time I surf a big wave it feels like the first time I went surfing when I was younger. I'm enjoying every second!

As soon as you catch the wave, you are living in the moment. It's a crazy feeling to be connected with the ocean, the wave, your board, body and mind in this way. You're a tiny object on the water and you feel like you're in the right place at the right time. I really enjoy this moment when riding a wave, and at the end I have a giant smile on my face as I know that I did all the right things at the right time.

One thing I've learned that really makes me more efficient and focused in the water while surfing big waves is to be more connected with my senses. When I enter the water, I can feel the temperature. I can taste the salt and see the colour of the wave. I can hear the birds. I really focus on my senses because if you can connect with your senses, you will be fully in the present.

In spots like Nazaré or Jaws, for example, when I'm waiting for a big wave, I start to feel the pressure and nerves. You know there is a risk, and this almost gives you another sense because being afraid gives an affirmation to my body, which automatically helps it find extra focus.

As soon as I feel these emotions, I focus on my breathing, being aware of the water, the air, and all my surroundings. I'm more aware than ever to stay on my feet and not fall.

— "

Justine's ability to be fully present isn't just reserved for big wave surfing.

" —

An example of a time that living in the present and enjoying the moment helped me was when I went to the World SUP and Paddleboard Championships in El Salvador in 2019. My only goal was to win, so I had this pressure on me. I can still remember everything because I was so focused and living in the moment. It was so much better for me, and I really felt the energy of being connected with the ocean and with nature. It made the victory all the more memorable.

— "

YORK'S NOTES

Having doubts and feeling fear are completely normal emotions that we all experience in everyday situations, and it's no different for Justine when she's about to ride a 70-foot wave. Through her experience, Justine has trained herself to react positively in these situations and move forwards with poise and confidence. She has the self-awareness to connect with her senses and the environment around her, which brings her into the present moment. Our senses are such a powerful tool, and the way Justine is able to be so descriptive about hers provides a fascinating insight into what it's like out on the water. By living in the moment, Justine can enjoy every second of the ride, just like she did the first time she jumped on a surfboard as a youngster.

YORK'S EXERCISE

BEING IN THE MOMENT CAN HELP YOU EXPERIENCE REAL ***SATISFACTION IN WHAT YOU'RE DOING.*** HERE'S A FRAMEWORK THAT CAN HELP YOU GET THERE:

1

This might seem hard, but the next time you're a couple of days ahead of a **moment or an event** where something is **at stake** – if you're taking a test, for example, or delivering a presentation at work – try to put the potential outcomes **to one side** for a minute and **concentrate** on the **journey** that **brought you there.**

Ask yourself questions like these:

- How much **effort** have you put into getting to this moment?
- What have you **learned** along the way?
- Have you already **achieved** part of the goal by making it this far?
- Are you the **only** person responsible, or have you worked as part of a **team?**
- Do you feel it's a **privilege** to simply be in this situation, something that a lot of other people will **not** get to experience?

When you're considering the answers, see if you can find **satisfaction** in the journey to date – in what you've **learned** from all that **revision,** or the **experiences** so far.

You have more **control** over the **process** than the **outcome,** so by allowing yourself to take a **step back** from the eventual result, you're giving yourself the best **opportunity** to experience regular **enjoyment along the way** rather than satisfaction only at the **end.**

Just before the test or presentation starts, try to **"be"** in the moment by **mindfully paying attention** to all your **senses** – take in the **smells,** the **sights,** and the **sounds** of your environment. Hopefully, you'll be able to **approach** your current situation with added **motivation** and **joy.**

YOUR NOTES

CHAPTER 2

BUILDING SUPPORT NETWORKS

INTRODUCTION

A COMMON LEARNING FROM THE ATHLETES FEATURED IN THIS BOOK IS THAT THEY DIDN'T ACHIEVE THEIR GOALS ALL BY THEMSELVES. SURE, THEY ALL HAD TO PERFORM INDIVIDUALLY IN KEY MOMENTS, BUT THEY WERE SUPPORTED EVERY STEP OF THE WAY BY A TRUSTED NETWORK AROUND THEM.

IN THIS CHAPTER WE'LL LOOK AT:

- **Adapting to a new environment**
- **Trusting your people**
- **Building a special relationship**

WE'LL HEAR FROM:

Xavi Simons
"Having my family behind me and knowing they always supported me and that I could talk about everything with them, not just about football, but about life – that's been really important for me."

Sébastien 'Ceb' Debs
"Moments will come when you're tempted to not trust someone, to be selfish, thinking that it's your moment, your life, and that you want to be in control of your own fate, but that's a dysfunctional team."

Kristian Blummenfelt
"One of the reasons why we work so well together is because we are very like-minded. We have the same mentality in terms of being able to set goals and be dedicated towards them."

Before we get started, have a think about these questions: What does a supportive environment look like for you? And who is it that helps you be the very best version of yourself? Is it a mentor of some kind? A family member? A friend? Bear those questions in mind as you continue through the chapter, and we'll come back to them as we tackle the exercise at the end.

For so many athletes, having a supportive environment is a crucial part of their success. Knowing that they have the full support of their network and inner circle helps give them the confidence to take on new challenges and be more ambitious in terms of goal setting.

Having that kind of support network can make all the difference in our daily lives as well. Through feeling a sense of belonging to a group that accepts, trusts, and values us, we're more likely to be able to believe we can achieve whatever we set our minds to.

Three elite athletes are featured in this chapter, who have all benefited from strong and supportive networks during their careers. Let's uncover a bit more about what they've learned on their journeys.

> *I'M NOT GOING TO SAY IT WASN'T HARD TO COME INTO A NEW ENVIRONMENT, WITH NEW PEOPLE.*

F*** THE LIMITS

S3, EP 1

LISTEN TO THE PODCAST HERE:

XAVI SIMONS

A GAME-CHANGING PRESENCE FOR CLUB AND COUNTRY, XAVI SIMONS IS A PRECOCIOUS FOOTBALLING TALENT WHO WAS SCOUTED BY BARCELONA AT THE AGE OF JUST SIX.

By the time he was 14, Xavi had more than a million Instagram followers and had starred in an advert alongside Neymar Jr and Ronaldinho. In 2022, he became the youngest Dutchman to play in a World Cup knockout game and he has progressed to become one of the most sought-after offensive players in Europe – especially after a series of eye-catching performances at Euro 2024, including a stunning goal against England in the semi-finals.

At club level, he has already played for Paris Saint-Germain and PSV Eindhoven and is currently enjoying life in the Bundesliga at RB Leipzig. So, when he speaks about the challenges of joining a new team, he really knows what he's talking about!

Here, he explains how he benefits from the psychological support in place at the club, his fellow professionals, and his family.

"

In professional football, when you go to a new club or you go to a new environment, you have to be right there at your top level in a matter of moments. It's the world of football. Nobody's going to say, "You're a new player here, so I'll give you one or two months to adapt." You have a couple of weeks to be with a new group and then you just have to perform.

When I joined RB Leipzig, I was here for two or three weeks of training, playing games, and then immediately we had the Super Cup final against Bayern Munich. It's very important for the club, so you have to be at the level.

When I arrived, they explained the role that everyone has at the club. I met the mental coach, Dr Peter Schneider, and we now see each other every day, and we speak about everything. Not only with Pete, but with a lot of people at the club; we always talk about the mindset and how it can improve the performance at the weekend.

Having a good environment during the week is really important. Mental coaches are something new to the world of football but, especially for me, it's so important to have a good mindset, to come to the club every day and enjoy being there.

I'm not going to say it wasn't hard at the time, to come into a new environment with new people. I was lucky because I knew a few players already from before, but when you come, and you go straight on to the big stage, at the same time as you're trying to adapt yourself to the people and the communication, it's hard.

On a personal level, I was determined to have good relationships with the guys, while being ready to show them that on the pitch I was ready to play that Super Cup game. I just made up my mind to go for it, and it went well, and we won 3-0.

In football, you have 24 hours of pressure and then, when you go back in the dressing room after training, you want to enjoy your time with the guys. And there are little things, like playing Uno – we play ping-pong as well – that help our mind to be calm and to relax and enjoy ourselves.

But even then, it's hard, especially if you're alone. Like at the start, I was alone in a hotel, before I had a house. You go to the club, the hotel, and then you're in a room and you can feel like you're going to go crazy.

— ”

Xavi has grown up with the pressures of the game, having been in the spotlight since a young age, but his family have been with him every step of the way to help him cope with the demands.

“ —

My dream has always been to play football, but I didn't want to be famous. I didn't even know what that was! Being such a talent at 13 years old meant people expected a lot of things from me, which was good, but at the same time, people can judge you as well and have no problem talking about you.

So having my family behind me and knowing they always supported me and that I could talk about everything with them, not just about football, but about life – that's been really important for me. The fact that I have the mindset I have nowadays is because of them.

That's especially the case with my older brother, having him with me and beside me, and going home and him saying to me, "We don't talk about football; we talk about life."

He has shown me that not everything in life is football.

— ”

Everyone will be able to relate to the kind of first-day nerves Xavi talks about – and especially the time it takes to adapt to a new culture and figure out how you fit into the group. Particularly when you factor in a move to another country, it can be extremely lonely. That's why it's really important to call on friends and family at these times because not only can they give you comfort, but they can also provide perspective – like Xavi's brother reminding him that not everything in life is about football. It must have been helpful, too, being able to socialise with his new teammates. He was lucky enough to know some of them already, but he made a point of getting to know others by relaxing with them off the pitch. Finding ways to connect with a new team can help you feel more at ease, and well placed to flourish in a new environment.

SÉBASTIEN 'CEB' DEBS

CEB HAS HAD AN INTEGRAL ROLE IN DEVELOPING ONE OF THE MOST SUCCESSFUL TEAMS IN THE WORLD OF GAMING – OG ESPORTS.

Initially joining as a coach of the Dota 2 team in 2016, Ceb transitioned to a playing role two years later and his presence inspired OG Esports to consecutive victories at The International, one of the world's most prestigious tournaments.

The Frenchman believes the driving force behind OG's ability to perform at their best under the most intense pressure was down to one core quality – trust. Without the highest level of trust, it would have been impossible for the team to thrive and achieve their goals.

Let's go behind the scenes with OG Esports and learn about the environment the team created. Oh, and if you're not a gaming expert and don't know what a "hero" is, think of it as the main character or persona that the team chooses to play.

"

When you're part of a top team in Dota, you spend most of the time with your teammates. We meet up in training centres and spend weeks and months together. Trust is everything. You've got to show your teammates they can trust you. There's so much pressure. Moments will come when you're tempted to not trust someone, to be selfish, thinking that it's your moment, your life, and that you want to be in control of your own fate, but that makes for a dysfunctional team.

I had to work really hard on letting go throughout my career. Dota is the thing that I care the most about in my life, but I've learned to let it go and fully trust other people. At The International in 2018, we were playing the grand finals. It's a best of five and we were 2-1 down, playing in game four. If we lost, we were out. We're selecting our strategy before the game begins, it's the very last pick and it's my choice of hero. There is a hero that we practised with only twice, and both times it went awful, but I had a strong feeling this is the game for it. I called for that hero, and I expected a reaction of, "Come on, are you sure?" from my teammates. They had all the reason in the world to freak out, but I got complete trust. I had no sense even for a second that they doubted me.

I got a sense of hype and excitement from them, and it sent my confidence through the roof. The game was really hard, but I put a lot of groundwork in with that hero and we ended up bringing it back.

In order to compete at the highest level, there needs to be a safe space – the highest level of trust. It's not only in the game, but also outside the game too. You've got to know they're going to be there for you, just like you're going to be there for them. If I have a problem during my day, are you going to help me out? If it's the weekend and we're off, can I count on you if I give you a call?

This is often underrated, but the connection has to be built, and it has to be very solid. Every opportunity to push the bond even further to emphasise the connection should be taken in a team – whatever makes you feel that I'm going to be

there for you and that you can count on me when it matters. I kept trying to be a better teammate and improving myself over the years even though I was failing. I kept trying and kept working on myself, and that was the real success.

series
Red Bull
OG

YORK'S NOTES

OG Esports sounds like a team everyone would love to be a part of! The way they explicitly trusted each other to perform at their best when it really mattered filled them all with so much confidence. This then allowed them to shine as individuals, which in turn elevated the overall team performance to levels they didn't know they could reach. As Ceb points out, a team that doesn't trust each other can quickly turn dysfunctional, so it must have been very rewarding for him to be at the heart of cultivating this positive atmosphere. Telling our teammates we trust them is something we can all remember to do in the future. It doesn't have to be the whole team straight away, either. You can start by forming a bond of trust with just one other person. You can then bring more and more people in as time goes on.

> I REALISED I HAD TO COMBINE MY PHYSICAL SHAPE WITH MY COACH'S DATA AND KNOWLEDGE. I KNEW IT COULD CREATE SOMETHING GREAT IN THE MIDDLE.

S3, EP 6

LISTEN TO THE PODCAST HERE:

KRISTIAN BLUMMENFELT

THE NORWEGIAN CHAMPION TRIATHLETE IS ON A MISSION TO PUSH THE LIMITS OF PEAK HUMAN PERFORMANCE.

Kristian's vision is shared by his coach Olav Aleksander Bu, who we'll also hear from in a Q&A at the end of this chapter. Olav is a sports scientist who has been instrumental in preparing Kristian both mentally and physically for the brutal nature of the sport since they first started working together in 2016.

In combining Kristian's physical capabilities with Olav's scientific and data-driven approach, the duo has redefined what was previously thought possible in their sport. This culminated in 2022 when, already a World, Olympic, and IRONMAN champion, Kristian became the first person to complete a sub-seven-hour Iron Distance triathlon.

The positive relationship between athlete and coach has been key in Kristian's achievements on the global stage.

“ —

There are very few people so extremely into what they are doing as Olav. He has seven different lives! Typically, when you work with a coach, it's a former athlete that has turned into a coach, but Olav has so many different experiences. He's a very good person to be around and he teaches me a lot.

One of the reasons why we work so well together is because we are very like-minded. We have the same mentality in terms of being able to set goals and being dedicated towards them.

I never used to think too much about physics and data. I thought I could just tolerate the pain better than others and deal with more lactic acid. But when I started to understand more about the data Olav showed me from the lab and the testing we do, I realised I had to combine my physical shape with his data and knowledge. If we combined the two, I knew it could create something great in the middle.

Before an IRONMAN, it's nerve-wracking even as a professional. You know that even if you have your best day, it's going to be eight hours of racing, and you'll hit the wall with 15–20 kilometres left, and you have to run through it.

No matter how well you pace yourself, you know it's going to be a long day. You know this beforehand, as do all the other athletes. It's not a walk in the park; it's going to be brutal. You feel nerves, the intensity, and that you have a full day of racing ahead of you. You're trying to enjoy the moment, while also being a bit afraid.

Typically, it's in the three weeks leading into a race where Olav will be giving me and my teammate the most feedback. He'll be helping us not just with the training programme, but also analysing the course and looking at data to give us as much information as possible.

We'll get out on the course to get a sense of how it feels, and he can tell us what the conditions will be like on race day and calculate if we'll be going faster or slower than we did in training, or in the race last year.

Based on data like this, we can get a feeling of what's required on race day. For example, before I did my first ever half IRONMAN distance, we looked at the bike split from the athlete who won the year before. Olav gave me a power wattage that I had to hold in order to be able to ride with him if he was riding at the same pace.

We figured out it was too optimistic, so we reduced my target power by 20 watts, knowing I'd then be two minutes behind him going into the run. We felt I could survive this and that I could catch up. When race day came, I let the guy disappear on the bike and I got in two minutes behind him as predicted. Then, also as predicted, I was able to take him on the run. So, based on the numbers that Olav was able to give me in advance, it made it easier for me to be confident for race day.

"

YORK'S NOTES

The relationship between athlete and coach is always going to be a key factor for success. Kristian and Olav have an overarching mission to push human performance, break boundaries, and show other people what's possible. In a sport like IRONMAN, you definitely need to have this extremely high level of dedication and commitment from both the coach and the athlete. With the number of hours they train, it's difficult to even imagine what that type of life is like. When it comes to the performance of Kristian, they're trying to control all the physical parameters that are humanly possible to control so that Kristian has the highest potential of anyone on the starting line to complete the triathlon in the fastest possible time. This is a really strong way of finding and building confidence.

YORK'S EXERCISE

IN THIS EXERCISE, TRY TO THINK ABOUT SUPPORT FROM ***TWO*** DIFFERENT POINTS OF VIEW – SO NOT JUST HOW ***YOU CAN FEEL*** MORE SUPPORTED IN YOUR ***DAY-TO-DAY LIFE***, BUT HOW YOU CAN DO YOUR BEST TO ENSURE YOU ARE OFFERING SUPPORT TO ***OTHERS TOO.***

1

Think of a time when you felt **confident, comfortable,** and **supported.** Maybe it was during a sporting competition of some kind, with your coach and teammates beside you, or when you were playing or singing in a band, working closely with a colleague on a particular project, or gaming with your friends.

Dive into this moment and think not just about how you **felt,** but also about the particular **aspects** of the **setting** that made you feel supported. Did someone do something that you especially **appreciated** – giving you a kind word, keeping eye contact, or making a physical gesture of some sort?

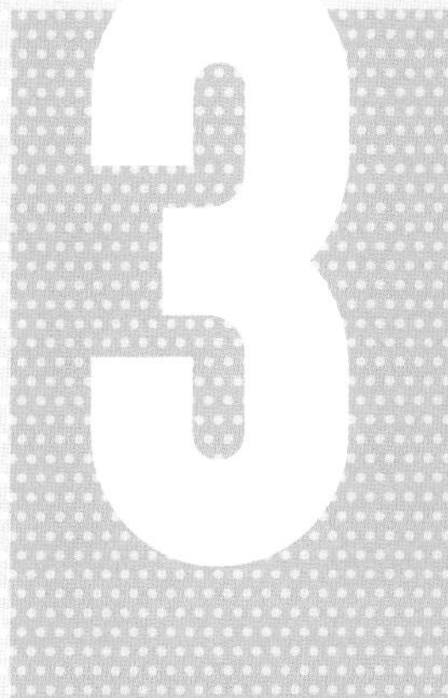

3

Now, think of a moment when you **didn't** feel particularly supported – for example, during a class or at a work meeting, when something went **wrong,** or you felt like you were being **unfairly** singled out for **criticism.**

4

What was it about the situation that made you feel **unsupported?** If you were giving a presentation that didn't go so well, were your colleagues giving you their full **concentration,** or just looking **at their phones?** If you were being criticised, did **no one** say anything to back you up? How about **afterwards** – did you look in vain for supportive **messages** or **texts?**

5

It's worth taking some **time** to **think** about how you have **reacted** when other people have been in **similar situations.** Have you been **guilty** of being on your phone when a friend has been in the spotlight and could have used your **full attention?** Have you always taken the **time** to seek out your colleagues and give them a **kind word** after a **difficult** experience?

6

One of the best ways of creating a **supportive environment** for yourself is to **ensure** you are **actively involved** in supporting others. That goes for the workplace, at college, or in clubs and teams: if you can get into the **habit** of **playing that role** of the supportive person, you'll help **generate** an atmosphere of **mutual trust.** You **shouldn't** feel like you always have to give advice or provide a solution to every problem; often, just **being there** to listen is **enough.**

7

The other side of this is to remember **it's fine** to go ahead and **ask for** the support you require. Do you need to feel that people are paying attention when you are making a presentation? **Tell** your closest colleagues! And crucially, make sure you **do the same** for them too!

Q&A OLAV ALEKSANDER BU

Behind two of the world's greatest triathletes, Norwegians Kristian Blummenfelt and Gustav Iden, stands a coach and sports scientist renowned for his data-driven approach to high performance.

Olav Aleksander Bu grew up on a farm where he developed a fascination for how technology works, tearing things apart then putting them back together again. With a background in electronics and a degree in engineering, Olav has pioneered a programme in men's triathlon that has resulted in a slew of major accolades.

He joined us for the interview with IRONMAN and Olympic triathlon champ Kristian Blummenfelt to talk about their relationship, and the lengths they go to in order to first gather, and then understand, the vast amount of data they use to help in preparation and performance.

How would you describe your relationship with Kristian?

What I really enjoy with Kristian is that I view us, not as one guy above the other or, let's say, the coach with the athlete below. I continuously learn from Kristian as well. He is one of the guys who I know will come back with reflections later; he will even spend his rest day starting to read something or dig into something, because it catches his interest.

But of course, we can't forget that the reason we are here is because of performance and this extreme dedication and belief in the ability to perform. For me, it's important that I really push the limits for everything I do in the same way that he does in racing and training. I think that energy and that dedication to what we do is combined in a common goal.

I don't say this to be nice to him, but I have yet to meet anyone else with Kristian's mindset when it comes to performance – that's something which has never ceased to amaze me.

I HAVE YET TO MEET ANYONE ELSE WITH KRISTIAN'S MINDSET WHEN IT COMES TO PERFORMANCE – THAT'S SOME-THING WHICH HAS NEVER CEASED TO AMAZE ME.

With Kristian, you've broken all the records – where do you go from here?

It's going back and just doing everything one more time. It's a tough thing to motivate yourself for, but we have learned so much together through all these years that we've become more and more aware of a project we have dubbed Finding Peak Human Performance.

We know we have already exceeded what is established as truth in science – not by small margins, but massively so, and it never fails to amaze me that we are always pushing the boundaries. But when it's going to break, we really don't know, because we are already far beyond what is written in any textbook.

So we're basically writing the chapters. And I think this is what the Peak Human Performance Project is. It is truly an interesting journey to be part of, together with Kristian, exploring this and figuring out what the limits of performance are. I'm very fortunate to have a guy like this to work with, to be honest.

I THINK THE UNDERLYING MECHANISM, THE BASIS OF MOVING THINGS FORWARD, IS ALWAYS WANTING TO SEE IF WE CAN TAKE ONE MORE STEP, BEING CURIOUS, AND NOT BEING AFRAID OF MAKING ERRORS OR OF FAILURE.

How did you develop the unique approach you have to training?

Since I was a kid, I have always been very curious. I remember my grandfather calling me a philosopher before I started at primary school. At that time, I thought it was a bad thing to be a philosopher, but today I actually enjoy it because at some point, when you are trying to break barriers and you can't rely on books any more, you have to be able to sit down and philosophise and take a helicopter view, or start asking meta questions, such as, why do I think this way? Why should this be a limitation? Is it really a limitation?

I think the underlying mechanism, the basis of moving things forward, is always wanting to see if we can take one more step, being curious, and not being afraid of making errors or of failure.

This is something we talk about quite a bit. If we really want to be competitive, we must also have the mindset of the second best. What would the second-best guy be trying to do, if he wants to beat you? So, for example, how would Kristian, if he were in second position, out-compete himself?

If things don't go to plan in the run-up to a big race, how do you adjust and cope?

Kristian is quite good at coming to terms with the situation. So even if things are horrible, he may get irritated or frustrated, but then he sucks it up, focuses on the goal, and makes the best of the situation. And that is something I really enjoy; it makes it really easy to work with him.

If you stress out and spend so much energy focusing on everything that is wrong and all the things that you should have done and that you can't do anything about, then everything becomes about damage control.

But we have learned to believe in ourselves, and we know that stressing out – we can't do anything with that. So we write it down as a lesson learned and take it with us after the race into the next one. But the start line is the time to focus only on what we are able to.

So, for me, the last week leading into the race is not about data or the programme any more; it's about Kristian's comfort and what he feels needs to be done.

WE HAVE LEARNED TO BELIEVE IN OURSELVES, AND WE KNOW THAT STRESSING OUT – WE CAN'T DO ANYTHING WITH THAT.

How involved does Kristian get in the data side of things?

We have worked such a long time together that Kristian is really, really good with data. I'm confident that he would easily be able to take a PhD in physiology if that was what he wanted to do.

Some people find their passion in academia, and he finds his passion in sport, but with an extremely strong mind and the ability to understand everything. So it's not like I have to tell him, "You should do maybe a little bit more like this."

He will have such a good understanding that my job is then to make sure he can focus on what is important for him and to take away all the surrounding stress. And hopefully, we have set things up in such a good way that the days leading up to the race are a breeze.

THE DATA CAN ACT AS A POSITIVE REINFORCEMENT LOOP, BECAUSE THERE ARE MANY TIMES I ASK MYSELF, AM I DOING GOOD ENOUGH?

How does having all the data help with mindset?

The data can act as a positive reinforcement loop, because there are many times I ask myself, am I doing good enough? And I think getting confirmation back that I am – that is important. And when you're using data in a good way – you feel that this seems like a good performance and you have data to reinforce this – it is a strong psychological combo for building confidence. And it's not superficial confidence, where you think, "Oh yeah, I'm on a good run, I'm so good", but you also get hard facts that support your feelings. That is where data can be used to supercharge the mental aspect as well.

YOU ALSO GET HARD FACTS THAT SUPPORT YOUR FEELINGS. THAT IS WHERE DATA CAN BE USED TO SUPERCHARGE THE MENTAL ASPECT AS WELL.

As well as the data, how important are the relationships you build with people in your team?

I need to care for the people I work with. Even though you sometimes have to be very clear about the direction in which things have to go, I am always aware of the people, because that's what I think is important for long-term performance.

You can, maybe, extract more from people in the short term by being very, let's say, harsh or direct, but I think that is a short-lived strategy. To have people really flourish and perform all the time, you have to create an environment where they feel they can flourish or perform.

CHAPTER 3

FACING YOUR FEARS

INTRODUCTION

FEAR IS PART OF BEING HUMAN, AND EVERYONE DEALS WITH IT IN SOME FORM. IN FACT, WE COULD PROBABLY ALL THINK OF A MOMENT RIGHT NOW WHEN WE'VE FELT FEAR AND REMEMBER EXACTLY WHAT THE EXPERIENCE WAS LIKE.

IN THIS CHAPTER WE'LL LOOK AT:

Having a courage mindset

Making fear your best friend

Fear of people's opinions

WE'LL HEAR FROM:

Emil Johansson
"As humans, we're all born with a gift. What you decide to do with that is what separates people from one another."

Dario Costa
"What I added was the respect for fear. I started to listen to my fears and make them my best friends."

Dr Michael Gervais
"If you can train your mind to create enough space to be in the present moment, the whole world changes."

Maybe you recall your heart beating that little bit faster, and your palms starting to sweat as you were confronted with a situation that made you feel vulnerable. You might even have the feeling of being able to taste what it was like.

Fear can prevent us from undertaking daily tasks like presenting in front of a big audience at work or having a difficult conversation with a friend or family member.

But it doesn't have to be that way. As the high performers featured in this chapter have all shown in their different ways, fear can also be a superpower – as long as we're prepared to face it rather than run away from it. By acknowledging fear, and learning to understand it, we can develop the courage to grow as an individual, learn new skills, and become the best version of ourselves.

We spoke to three elite individuals who know the true meaning of fear and have embraced it to harness their emotions for a better performance. So, let's find out how to turn fear... into fuel.

> *I BELIEVE ONE OF MY BIGGEST MENTAL STRENGTHS IS THE COURAGE OF BELIEVING IN MYSELF AND NOT SECOND-GUESSING MYSELF.*

S2, EP 11

LISTEN TO THE PODCAST HERE:

EMIL JOHANSSON

IF YOU LOVE RIDING BIKES DOWN BIG HILLS, EMIL JOHANSSON LIKELY NEEDS NO INTRODUCTION.

For those of us who don't follow mountain biking, the easiest way of describing Emil Johansson is that the Swede is the most successful slopestyle rider in the history of the sport.

A Triple Crown of Slopestyle winner on three occasions, Emil has mastered the art of being comfortable in uncomfortable situations. Key to his success is having the courage to trust his instincts and always believe in himself.

He rides the kind of lines that come from being in control, not out of it – and it all starts not from conquering his fear, but from a different approach: accepting it.

"

I stuck with biking because my brain could wire it, and that's what got me hooked. In life, it's always a matter of finding answers to things. If you believe in what you want to do, and you don't feel like there's a stupid risk involved, you can just go and do it.

The fear is always there. Sometimes it has to do with the jump, sometimes it has to do with the trick you want to do on it, and sometimes it's everything combined. It depends how much you tune into it and how much you listen to it and how affected you feel. I always try to break it down and look at the reason behind this fear. Is there something I can do to get rid of it, or at least work my way around it?

It's so hard sometimes to break it down, and you're just stuck in the rut where it's scary and you don't really know how to get out of that position, but over time you get better at it.

Even though we're doing dangerous things, we're still very human. Over time, and with lots of preparation, we've got to the point where things that didn't used to be possible, are now possible.

I believe one of my biggest mental strengths is the courage of believing in myself and not second-guessing myself. That comes from years of a lot of trial and error and getting to the point where I'm confident that my instincts are correct, and that I can trust my thought process.

As humans, we're all born with a gift. What you decide to do with that is what separates people from one another.

YORK'S NOTES

Emil is very reflective about the processes he goes through, and very rational in his thinking. Even though what he does can be dangerous, there's always a process behind it that means he feels safe. For Emil, courage often comes from answering a series of questions in advance of doing something, questions like: Is the trick even possible? What are the potential risks of doing it? What could go wrong? It's also interesting to highlight that, for Emil, it's not about removing the fear. When he's about to send a big jump and complex trick, he'll still have fear, but, crucially, he's done all the preparation beforehand. That, it turns out, can be incredibly empowering.

DARIO COSTA

THE HISTORY-MAKING AEROBATIC PILOT CONTINUES TO PUSH THE BOUNDARIES OF WHAT'S POSSIBLE IN A PLANE.

In September 2021 Dario Costa wowed viewers around the world with his 44-second flight through two tunnels in Istanbul. The speed of that flight? Close to 300 kilometres an hour. The margin for error? Basically zero.

Tunnel Pass was one of the most impressive feats of pure focus in human history and because training for it couldn't involve real-life practice, Dario had to prepare in other ways. To cement his place in the aviation record books, Dario had to not only move past his fear but actually use it as a tool to direct his focus and training. Here's how the Red Bull Air Race veteran explains the process.

"

When you're part of something pioneering, your mindset has to completely change. Where before you were following rules, now you have to help create rules.

My idea was to take off from one tunnel, fly out of it, and entirely through another one. I had to learn every single centimetre of the tunnel and I couldn't move my eyes. When you move your eyes at 300 kilometres an hour in such a machine, you go where your eyes go.

Everything was planned and visualised without using any simulators. I was told I had to react in 250 milliseconds or less, otherwise I would crash.

I had no margin for error. What I added was the respect for fear. I started to listen to my fears and make them my best friends.

I started to have my fears suggest to me what I had to mitigate. I started to talk to my fears instead of doing what most of the people say, which is to ignore your fears. They say things like, "Have no fear!" This is stupid. If I had no fear, I would not be here talking to you. What I suggest is to listen to your fears, understand what they're suggesting to you because our fears are based on our experiences.

The moment I started the engine, my fear stopped distracting me. I was doing what I was expecting.

I want to push the boundaries of my comfort zone because it means I'm creating something that was never done before.

It's a rule I have in my life: if you don't get out of your comfort zone, you're not creating. And I want to create.

"

> I HAD NO MARGIN FOR ERROR. WHAT I ADDED WAS THE RESPECT FOR FEAR. I STARTED TO LISTEN TO MY FEARS AND MAKE THEM MY BEST FRIENDS.

S1, EP 14

LISTEN TO THE PODCAST HERE:

Red Bull

YORK'S NOTES

The Tunnel Pass project required Dario to overcome not just one fear but many – fear of making a mistake, fear of failure, fear of crashing. It was an intense environment with literally zero room for error. Pushing the limits of your comfort zone is a critical skill in pursuing a worthy goal, and Dario's achievement illustrates that we're moving in and out of our comfort zones all the time. When we're in a safe and familiar environment or headspace, we feel that we can control what happens to us, but it can also lead us to miss out on a lot of experiences and opportunities.
It's only when we enter a world of uncertainty that the fear sets in, but we can work with it and use it to help us achieve our dreams. At the end of this chapter, we'll try an exercise to help you react positively in a situation that requires you to move forwards out of your comfort zone.

> THE GREATEST CONSTRICTOR OF OUR POTENTIAL IS THIS UNPRODUCT-IVE OBSESSION WITH BEING OK IN THE EYES OF OTHERS.

S3, EP 11

LISTEN TO THE PODCAST HERE:

DR MICHAEL GERVAIS

RENOWNED PSYCHOLOGIST MICHAEL GERVAIS IS A LEADING EXPERT ON THE RELATIONSHIP BETWEEN THE MIND AND HUMAN PERFORMANCE.

As a high-performance psychologist, Michael's clients have ranged from corporate CEOs to some of the world's most successful athletes.

And he's no stranger to high-stakes moments, having coached Felix Baumgartner ahead of his Red Bull Stratos space dive in 2012, an extraordinary freefall from the edge of space that made him the first human being to travel faster than the speed of sound outside a vehicle.

Michael joined us on *Mind Set Win* to give us some insights into his Finding Mastery techniques – and he had an interesting take on a preoccupation that most of us can probably relate to: Fear of People's Opinions.

"

My idea of FOPO was inspired by FOMO, fear of missing out. When I read that, I was like, "Oh, I recognise that!" And then I thought, that's not my real fear. I've got a fear that is a little different, which is the fear of people's opinions.

When I was 16, I was a good little surfer but come competition days, I was a disaster. As soon as there were judges and family and friends and people that were evaluating me, I was a shell of myself. It was like I could access just about 50 per cent of what I was capable of.

So, I'm in a heat and this competitor paddles by me and he says, "Gervais, I surf with you every day out here. You've got to stop worrying about all the things that could go wrong." And I thought, how does he know? That's exactly what's going on inside. So, then I thought, well, OK, so that's not working.

What would work? This is a simple 16-year-old's line: Let me start thinking about what could go right! I don't know what happened, but it started to work. And I thought to myself, what just happened? My physical skill didn't change. My technical skills didn't change, but I changed my mind.

Then later on, I was working with professional athletes, and it showed up with them too – this fear of not wanting to let people down, not wanting to blow it for their agent, for their mom, for their dad, for their boys, for their teammates.

I think the greatest constrictor of our potential is this unproductive obsession with being OK in the eyes of others.

Our thoughts directly impact our emotions, and our emotions and our thoughts together create a feeling. And it's that feeling, that we're trying to be connected to something or share something, that is essential for high performance. What your thoughts can do is, they're either creating constriction or some space.

When you create more space, in the way that you're thinking to yourself about yourself, about the task at hand, it allows you to slip into the present moment and once you're on time with the unfolding present moment, you give yourself a chance.
I can't overstate how important the practice of being present is.

You're giving yourself a chance because high performance happens in the present moment. And so, part of the math of this whole psychology game is to increase the amount of time that you're actually in the present moment, and if you can train your mind to create enough space to be in the present moment, the whole world changes.

YORK'S NOTES

Being fearful of what others think of us can really affect our self-confidence and make us concentrate on the things that could go wrong. What if I can't remember the answer? What if I'm not good enough? What if they don't like me? These worries can quickly become overwhelming and make you feel as though your whole identity is on the line. Michael's way of combating FOPO is to keep it simple. Concentrating on the tasks at hand – tying your laces, catching a wave, whatever it is – can really root you in the present moment, and free you of unhelpful distractions.

And for another way of tackling this, check out the exercise at the end of the chapter!

YORK'S EXERCISE

WHAT ATHLETES ***EMIL*** AND ***DARIO*** HAVE IN ***COMMON*** IS THAT, AT SOME POINT, THEY HAVE HAD TO ***ACCEPT*** AND ***EMBRACE*** THEIR FEARS AND EMOTIONS IN ORDER TO ***ACHIEVE*** THEIR ***GOALS.***

To help find a way we can all do this, we're introducing a psychological approach rooted in Eastern philosophy that's based around mindfulness, acceptance, and commitment (MAC). It's a very popular practice in everyday life psychology that can help us all regulate our emotions and enhance our daily performance and wellbeing.

The MAC approach has also been applied and adapted specifically for sport performance by many people, including the people who developed it, Frank Gardner and Zella Moore. Here's an overview to learning and actioning it at home.

1

Mindfulness

The all-important first step, this is where you have to learn to **acknowledge the emotion** you're feeling. Try to **practise** specifically labelling your emotions throughout the day. Give it a try at home – it's **harder** than you think! Can you feel the **difference** between fear, anger, frustration, and disappointment for example?

Acceptance

After acknowledging an emotion, you can learn to **accept it.** Remember here, emotions are a completely **natural response** of the body. Try to understand where the emotion **came from,** and what the **reasons** are behind it coming up inside of you. It's very important, however, that you don't **judge** the emotion or label it as something **good** or **bad.** You are just **experiencing** it and **noticing** it, but have no **subjective interpretation** of it.

Commitment

This is where you take **action** and start to **work** with the emotion. Over time, it will become a **habit** that you'll apply subconsciously if you practise it **often** enough. Maybe you decide to share your feelings with someone you trust, like a friend, partner, family member, or colleague. If you're nervous ahead of an exam for example, can you take action and **change** your preparation or revision schedule to **improve** how you are feeling?

Even though the aim is to **accept** the emotion as a natural consequence of the situation you are in, you still want to **take steps** to avoid something similar occurring in the future. So, **what steps** can you take to get yourself out of that situation? How can you **prevent** it happening again?

TO CONCLUDE, THERE ARE ***MANY WAYS*** TO LEARN ABOUT THIS APPROACH, SO FIND THE ***BEST ONE*** THAT WORKS ***FOR YOU.*** THERE ARE BOOKS, APPS, AND VIDEOS, AS WELL AS WORKSHOPS AND CLASSES, AS IT CAN BE PERFECTLY COMBINED WITH ACTIVITIES LIKE YOGA OR QIGONG.

CHAPTER 4

FINDING FLOW

INTRODUCTION

WHEN ATHLETES TALK ABOUT FINDING FLOW STATE, OR BEING IN THE ZONE, IT SOUNDS INCREDIBLE, RIGHT?

Flow is that semi-mythical state where you're totally relaxed, your body seems to know exactly what to do and your mind is able to react instinctively and effortlessly – making it possible to stretch yourself to the limits of your ability, while still feeling at ease and experiencing genuine enjoyment.

High-performance athletes often talk about reaching flow as becoming fully immersed in the moment, and they describe a point where awareness and action come together as one. Essentially, it is an optimal zone of functioning where you're highly concentrated, fully immersed in what you're doing, and performing at your peak – and it's not just high-performance athletes who can benefit from getting in the zone.

In fact, attaining flow is something we can experience in many different areas of our life – from personal problem-solving to clearing a backlog of work, or playing a musical instrument.

We can also think about flow state as a way of dealing with the distractions and demands we're constantly being bombarded with as part of modern life. If, like most of us, you find it hard to shut out emails, texts, social media notifications, the news, the noise, even your rumbling stomach ... then getting yourself in the zone is going to be a big help.

Of course, talking about flow state is a lot easier than actually achieving it – but the good news is that, with practice, we can all learn how to get there, and at the end of this chapter you'll find a really simple exercise that should be a big help in training yourself to get into the zone.

But first, let's hear from some athletes about their experiences of achieving flow – what it is for them, why it's important, and how they try to get there.

IN THIS CHAPTER WE'LL LOOK AT:

What is flow state

Hitting the sweet spot

Experiencing full immersion

WE'LL HEAR FROM:

Rhiannan Iffland
"It's like tunnel vision and a feeling of what I can only compare to hyperfocus."

Sam Sunderland
"I want to be on point, and the only way to do that is to get into a state of calmness."

Andrea Petkovic
"After the fourth point, I was in total flow state; I was just doing, being, existing in the moment."

> YOU KIND OF GET INTO THIS FLOW STATE. AND I'M STILL TRYING TO FIGURE OUT WHAT THAT PLACE IS, THAT I GO INTO WHEN I'M UP THERE. IT'S LIKE NOTHING ELSE. EVERYTHING JUST BOUNCES OFF YOU, ALL YOUR THOUGHTS.

RHIANNAN IFFLAND

AUSTRALIA'S RHIANNAN IFFLAND SEES THE WORLD DIFFERENTLY FROM MOST OTHER PEOPLE – FROM THE DIZZYING HEIGHTS OF RED BULL CLIFF DIVING, WHERE SHE IS THE MOST DOMINANT COMPETITOR THE SERIES HAS EVER KNOWN.

When it comes to high diving from a 21-metre platform, Rhiannan Iffland is the greatest to ever do it, having won the Red Bull Cliff Diving World Series eight times since her debut season in 2016.

In 2019, she rewrote the history books by winning every stop and achieving the perfect season – a feat she'd go on to repeat in 2021. A four-time champion in the World Aquatics high diving to boot, Rhiannan has well and truly cemented her legacy as the queen of the sport.

Key to her unrivalled consistency is her ability to stand on the platform and block out everything else in her mind that isn't related to her upcoming dive. Only by achieving this state of focus does she feel the energy and power she needs to perform at her best.

In this interview recorded especially for the *Mind Set Win* book, Rhiannan explains what finding her flow feels like before she's about to leap.

"

One of the biggest things about cliff diving is that when you're standing up there on the platform at that height; for me, everything just goes away, and that's the only thing on your mind.

You kind of get into this flow state. And I'm still trying to figure out what that place is, that I go into when I'm up there. It's like nothing else. Everything just bounces off you, all your thoughts. I'm only thinking about the dive.

It's like tunnel vision. It's super strange. It's a feeling of what I can only compare to hyperfocus. I feel an energy and a power that I never feel in any other place. It sounds strange, but it's so true. You're so focused that you feel this energy. And, for me, I try not to let any negative thoughts in; it's only positive, and I'm always telling myself: "This is your moment! Do it! Go for it!"

I can't explain it in any other way. And it's something that you don't remember either. Doing the dive is such a bizarre thing, because you do it, and you do it well, but sometimes you're like: "What just happened? I'm in the water already?" I'm still trying to figure it out.

I don't need to overthink the twists and flips. If you do it so many times in training, then this should just happen. It's about making the thoughts smaller, standing there, and focusing purely on two things, which, for me, could be: "Keep your head still; one and a half twists." Something so simple like that. I think it helps me get into that state as well, keeping it simple upstairs.

One thing that I've also noticed about myself is that if I'm walking up there with other divers, I generally don't like people talking into my ear, because I want to be thinking about what I'm doing. I don't like to be distracted because I lose focus quite easily.

I think most of the time [on the walk up to the platform], I'm only thinking about what I'm doing, so that once I do stand there, all the thoughts and all of the processes are already done, and it's go-time, when I can just focus on what I have to do. Every diver is different, but personally, I don't want to have a conversation about what we had for lunch on the way up to the platform."

YORK'S NOTES

Everyone experiences a flow state in a different way and it's therefore difficult to explain the antecedents, consequences, and sensations of it. Rhiannan does such a brilliant job of explaining what flow state feels like to her, which might be different to what it feels like to you. Having this image, feeling, and description of what flow feels like is so important, as visualising it can make it easier to find flow in the future. For Rhiannan, it's instinctive, effortless, and happens automatically when she's standing on the edge of the platform. Everything bounces off her, and she feels invincible. She also offered a great tip that's worth focusing on for a second – try to keep it simple. If you are focused too hard on the technicalities of what you're trying to do and have too many thoughts racing around your mind, you won't achieve flow. You need to let go of everything and be totally immersed in the present. If we can master this way of thinking, then we stand the best chance of finding our flow.

SAM SUNDERLAND

THE BRITISH RIDER IS A TWO-TIME WINNER OF THE DAKAR RALLY, MAYBE THE TOUGHEST MOTOR-SPORTS EVENT IN THE WORLD.

Alongside the physical challenges of riding thousands of kilometres over brutal terrain, winning the Dakar Rally means having the mindset to cope with the unpredictability, loneliness, sleep deprivation, and sheer chaos the race brings.

It sounds a formidable challenge but fortunately Sam's ability to find what he calls the sweet spot – and we might call flow – has made all the difference. Read on to discover exactly what he had to say about achieving this state of mind while coping with such physical and mental challenges.

" —

There's no way you can plan for the Dakar. You need to take what comes and be ready for the unexpected. There are multiple days, thousands of kilometres of sand, dunes, mountains, rocks, riverbeds, plateaus, and different weather.

You need to be ready, then take what comes, and quickly overcome and adapt to the situation thrown at you. Before the start of the stage are the last minutes before you're exposed to hours of chaos and unknowns. I quite like to stay quiet during these moments and just think about what I need to do. I don't like to talk too much and get distracted. I try to focus on what's coming.

Through my experiences over the years, I know that I need to be in a serious frame of mind because I know the consequences of a bad crash. For me, the only way to get there is to get into a state of calmness. If one second I'm talking to someone, the next second I'm doing stretches, the next I'm doing something else, it can put me in a different frame of mind before I set off. I like to have that little moment of quietness.

— "

> I HAVE TO GET INTO A STATE OF CALMNESS. IF MY EXCITEMENT IS TOO HIGH, MY PERFORMANCE GOES DOWN, IF MY EXCITEMENT ISN'T ENOUGH, MY PERFORMANCE GOES DOWN. I NEED TO BE IN A HAPPY MEDIUM.

S1, EP 15

LISTEN TO THE PODCAST HERE:

The British rider noticed earlier in his career that to perform at his best, his energy levels needed to be exactly right. It was through the help of a sports psychologist that he was able to understand how to identify where his levels were at during a race.

"

They showed me a graph with levels of excitement and performance on it. If my excitement is too high, my performance goes down, if my excitement isn't enough, my performance goes down. I've learned that I need to be in a happy medium.

Before a prologue, for example, I get so fired up that I'm almost shaking. In those moments, I try to picture where I am on the graph and, usually, I'm overexcited so I need to calm down a bit. I'll take some deep breaths and go off on my own, away from the chaos, and calm down.

The reverse is if I'm tired and didn't sleep well, I might not be excited enough, so I'll try to do some exercises to get my heart rate up. If I recognise that I'm too excited or too sleepy, I'll always think back to the graph and try to change it.

"

YORK'S NOTES

The graph Sam is talking about here is a model developed in the 1970s by psychologist Yuri Hanin called the individual zone of optimal functioning (IZOF). It helps Sam check where his levels of energy and anxiety are before a key stage of a race. What's vital to understand here is that we are all completely different in what we need in order to perform at our best. If Sam's overexcited and too energised, it will negatively impact his performance, but on the flip side, if he's a bit tired and not fully concentrating, he won't race to the best of his ability either. His optimal zone is somewhere in the middle. The way Sam is able to identify where he is on the graph, how he has developed techniques he can action in the moment in order to find his personal sweet spot, is very impressive.

AFTER ONE MATCH, I WAS SO IMMERSED IN THE EXPERIENCE THAT I DIDN'T REALISE I'D WON.... IT WAS LIKE SLIDING IN AND OUT OF A DREAM.

UNCUT, EP 21

LISTEN TO THE PODCAST HERE:

ANDREA PETKOVIC

THE GERMAN TENNIS PLAYER REACHED THE WORLD'S TOP 10 AND LIFTED SEVEN WTA TOUR SINGLES TITLES DURING HER CAREER, WHICH CAME TO AN END IN 2022 AFTER THE US OPEN.

Andrea's focus, competitiveness, and enthusiasm for the game made her one of the most popular and respected players of her era, and she relived every aspect of life as a tennis player when she came on to the show.

The decision to retire came at the age of 34, after many years of having a daily "battle of attrition" with her body. She describes her retirement as being like a grieving process, but once the decision was taken, she quickly found the freedom to explore new opportunities within the sport, like becoming a commentator. Here, she reflects on what it felt like when truly hitting the peaks and playing with true flow.

" —

There are different types of best matches. There are best matches where everything seems to be going your way, and it feels like you're in a casino and whatever you put on the roulette table wins and you can't even explain it. It's just happening that way.

Then you also have the type of matches that are not as easy in the beginning, but you find something inside yourself where all of a sudden everything seems to fall into place in the right way.

If we talk about mindset, both these types of matches have the flow state in common – a zone where you're not thinking about what you're doing and just being.

— "

The flow zone is what made Andrea really thrive on court and find her absolute peak performance level. She'd often experience this state of mind when up against an opponent who matched her shot for shot and pushed her to her limits.

" —

Your opponent has to be playing as well as you are because it becomes almost like a telepathic connection between the two of you.

It's like an unsaid truth that you're like, "OK, girl, you're playing well, I'm playing well, let's see who ends up winning this match in the end."

Those matches were my favourite, those really tight three-setters, where I came out on top but, in the process, it almost felt like it didn't matter who won the match. It was just a very real and true and pure battle between two people who tried their best to win.

— "

The key to living in this "beautiful place" is the ability to remove yourself from all the little thoughts and processes that constantly occur in your mind – at least, that was Andrea's experience against Maria Sharapova at the Australian Open in 2011, when she recorded a straight-sets victory over the multiple Grand Slam champion.

> My whole body was on full alert when I walked out. I was in the zone from the fourth point onwards and I never wavered. All the years of practice and training came to this pinnacle of this one match where everything just flowed out of me. I was just doing, being, existing in the moment.
>
> There is an image of me when I won the match: I turn around to the ball kid and I tell them to bring me my towel because I'm so immersed in this experience that I didn't even realise that the match was over. It took me 10 or 15 seconds to realise that I had won. And I think it was like sliding into a dream and then sliding out of a dream again.

YORK'S NOTES

There's no doubt that achieving a true flow state inspired Andrea to one of the standout victories of her career. She was so in the zone she didn't even realise the match was over! Andrea was facing a star of the sport in a packed stadium at the Australian Open, and this is an important factor to consider. While we can experience being in the zone for any task, true flow state occurs more frequently when we're under pressure and our body or mind is stretched to its limits. This doesn't just have to be in a sporting context. Did you ever take an exam and find yourself with one more question to answer with the clock ticking down? Something clicks into gear, and we're somehow able to find the focus to answer it in double-quick time? It's in these challenging moments of heightened stress that we fully engage in the task at hand and begin to forget everything else happening around us. The fear disappears and we can achieve things we never thought possible.

adidas
adidas

YORK'S EXERCISE

HOW CAN YOU CONSISTENTLY REACH ***FLOW STATE?*** OF COURSE, IT CAN BE CHALLENGING WITH ALL THE DEMANDS AND DISTRACTIONS HAPPENING ALL AROUND YOU IN DAILY LIFE, BUT THERE ARE SOME SIMPLE STEPS YOU CAN FOLLOW TO GIVE YOURSELF THE BEST OPPORTUNITY.

1

Having a **clear goal** in mind, something specific that you really want to achieve, is crucial in concentrating and **focusing the mind.** What are you currently working towards?

2

You're not going to reach flow state the first time you try it, so you need to **practise** in order to become familiar with whatever task you've chosen. Having an **image in your head** of what flow feels like can help here. What does it **taste** and **smell** like? What thoughts in your mind led you there in the past? The more tangible you can make it, the **easier** it is to **reach.**

Your thoughts and actions must remain **laser focused.** Tiredness, hunger, and thirst are all **distractions,** so make sure you've taken the necessary steps and sufficient breaks to ensure you can **maintain high concentration levels** and **avoid mental exhaustion.**

Don't let your mind **wander and flicker** between the **past** and the **present** moment. You need to stay entirely in the **present**. Remove all possible **distractions** by switching your phone and TV off. Also, try and be in a **calm space** away from other people or pets.

If you try and force finding your optimal zone of concentration, **you will fail!** You can't expect it to happen. Just like sleep, **if you actively try,** the chances are that it **won't work.**

Consistency is key, so it's really important to **practise** these techniques **daily.** The magic won't happen first time.

7

Remember, it's not **black and white.** You don't have to be in full flow state to be **productive.** Sometimes we experience **minor flow,** sometimes we have moments of **full immersion,** and sometimes it lasts for just **a few seconds.**

YOUR NOTES

CHAPTER 5

PREPARING TO SUCCEED

INTRODUCTION

ELITE ATHLETES OFTEN USE PRE-PERFORMANCE ROUTINES AS A TOOL TO HELP THEM SNAP INTO FOCUS AND COPE WITH THE PRESSURES OF AN UPCOMING PERFORMANCE.

IN THIS CHAPTER WE'LL LOOK AT:

Trusting in the process

The power of anchoring

Being ready to take your chance

WE'LL HEAR FROM:

Max Verstappen
"I have my routine, I work with my engineers, I do my work back at the factory, and I also trust the team around me to do their job to their best standards."

Marco Odermatt
"My brain has already skied these runs many times, so if I make a mistake, it knows exactly what to do next."

Liam Lawson
"I had the self-belief and knew I was ready for F1 but in this specific situation I was going to have one practice session on one of the hardest tracks on the calendar – and I knew the whole weekend was going to be wet."

By allowing themselves the time to prepare mentally and physically in a familiar environment, they're taking control of the situation and ensuring they're in the best state possible for what's about to unfold.

While this may sound ultra-professional, you really don't have to be a high-achieving athlete for a routine to help you prepare to succeed, as we all encounter moments when we need to be on high alert and fully focused – before a job interview, perhaps, or when giving a presentation, taking an exam, or playing sports. It doesn't matter if you're doing it for the first time or the 100th time, being fully prepared provides you with a moment of inner calm and the self-confidence that you've done everything you can to perform at your optimal level.

The fascinating thing about routines is that what works really well for one person might not work for somebody else. They're all unique to the individual and can include literally anything! Listening to your favourite music, a breathing exercise, visualisation, singing, yoga, talking, taking a walk in the fresh air – whatever works for you.

The common denominator is that your own optimal routine will act as an anchor, and repeating it every time you're confronted with a pressurised situation that requires focus can help bring positive results. At the end of the chapter, we'll return to the idea of creating an anchor routine, but for now let's look at the way three elite athletes make sure they're in an optimal state of readiness for their big moments.

MAX VERSTAPPEN

MAX'S ABILITY TO CONSISTENTLY DRIVE AT HIS PEAK LEVEL HAS HELPED HIM WIN RACE AFTER RACE FOR ORACLE RED BULL RACING.

In the minutes before a Formula 1 race, Max is calmness personified. Even in such a high-stakes sport where it feels like he's now expected to win every race, the multiple world champion can be found relaxing in his warm-up room and going with the flow.

Growing up, this kind of approach didn't always meet the approval of his F1 driver dad Jos Verstappen, but, for Max, staying chilled and trusting the process is the best way to blank out the pressure and prepare for the action that occurs when the lights go out.

And as the saying goes, if it ain't broke, don't fix it. After clinching his first World Championship title in dramatic circumstances in 2021, the Dutchman went from strength to strength to run away with the titles in 2022 and 2023, with the latter season featuring a record 19 race wins. He followed that up with his fourth world title in a row in 2024.

Here's how he explains his approach to race day.

" —

I enjoy what I'm doing, but I also don't make myself crazy. I don't put a lot of questions in my head. I just go with the flow, and this works for me.

Back in the day, I had a few arguments with my dad about it. He felt that I was always too relaxed. My dad is more into the lead-up of a Grand Prix and is more hyped-up than I am. For me, I only really get excited when I jump in the car.

I try to enjoy the moment that I'm in. I have my routine, I work with my engineers, I do my work back at the factory, and I also trust the team around me to do their job to their best standards."

— "

Alongside remaining carefree and calm, it's Max's simple pre-performance routine that helps him switch into gear and focus on the upcoming race. It takes place in his private driver's room at the paddock, often just minutes before the engines fire up.

" —

My routine depends a lot on what has happened already over the course of the weekend. The main part of my routine is always to warm up properly to fire up my body and brain step by step, to help get my muscles and reaction times on point.

There are a lot of things to analyse but the routine before I jump in the car is mainly just this, making sure I'm physically and mentally ready.

I can very easily switch into racing mode, and right up until the moment I leave to jump into the car, I can be relaxing and following all different sports.

— "

> YOU CAN'T HAVE OFF DAYS, OR OFF WEEKENDS; YOU HAVE TO BE ON IT ALL THE TIME. AND THAT'S NOT EASY TO ACHIEVE.

S2, EP 1

LISTEN TO THE PODCAST HERE:

F1's schedule – which in 2024 took in 24 races in 21 countries across five continents – is gruelling in the extreme, but Max has found an approach that provides him with the balance he needs to perform at his best and enjoy his success.

"

You can't have off days, or off weekends; you have to be on it all the time and that's not easy to achieve. For me personally, the laid-back, chilled approach helps me. I could stay for more hours at the track, but I don't think it helps my performance. F1 is a big part of my life but it's not everything. I don't need to be constantly thinking about it to perform. I know when to switch back on and when to switch off.

I don't like to overcomplicate or overthink things, as, for me, this doesn't work. I'm the sort of person who just enjoys what happens. I just want to enjoy the current moment, and I'll worry about what comes next later on.

"

YORK'S NOTES

Max's approach is a powerful reminder that if what you're doing is working, committing to it fully can result in long-term success. And if you know what works for you, why overcomplicate things? By resisting the temptation to drastically change his routine when something goes wrong, Max has been able to develop one of the core pillars of high performance – consistency. Consistency in his routine and mentality before a race brings consistency of performance during it. By trusting the process, his own skill, and the equally professional people around him, he has the optimal chance of doing what he does best – speeding around the track and taking the chequered flag.

MY ONLY ROUTINE IS THAT FOR 10 MINUTES BEFORE THE START GATE, I ALWAYS DO THE SAME THINGS.

MARCO ODERMATT

FEW ATHLETES HAVE DOMINATED THEIR SPORT AS COMPLETELY AS SWISS ALPINE SKIER MARCO ODERMATT IN RECENT TIMES.

Marco is the three-time reigning FIS overall champion and in 2024 he was virtually unbeatable. His 13 race victories across Super G, Downhill, and Giant Slalom saw him pick up the titles in all three disciplines. It was a season for the ages which, added to the fact he's the reigning Olympic and world champion, confirmed his status as an all-time great.

His dominance is built not only on the fact that he trains as hard as he races, but also on a 10-minute routine that helps him switch into gear before taking the start gate. Here, Marco explains just what he does in these crucial 10 minutes that make all the difference in finding that extra split second.

“ —

I think in every sport it's all about the preparation. In training, I really take the risks and go all in because my mind and body have to be in sync, so I can react the way I want to during a race. And if I make a mistake, I'm back on the line very quickly so I don't lose much time. If you really know what you want to do in every turn and every difficult passage, your body already knows what to do.

I'm really not the guy who has that many routines. I don't train or eat the same before every race for example. I'm very open minded in that regard. I think it's important to not be too fixed within yourself – I want to be relaxed and feel emotions for different things. My only routine is that for 10 minutes before the start gate, I always do the same things. I start with a warm-up, and then I visualise the track and have everything in my mind. I go through it over and over again.

My brain has already skied these runs many times, so if I make a mistake, it knows exactly what to do next. This is an important part for me.

Then, around three to four minutes before the race, I start thinking about some good memories and good thoughts. These are good for me to have in my mind.

— ”

It was this very routine that was the anchor that helped Marco overcome expectation, bad weather, and of course his rivals, to claim his first Olympic medal in Beijing in 2022.

“ —

In China, it all came down to my last chance in the Giant Slalom, where I was the big favourite. I had big pressure as I didn't have a medal yet. It wasn't meant to snow but we woke up in the morning to 20 centimetres of fresh snow. I was leading after the first run, but the second got delayed due to the bad weather, which you don't want.

I slept terribly and was so tired the whole day, so I took a nap between the two runs. I also planned to not go to the start area that early as it was so cold. Everyone was telling me to go to the start gate, but I took it easy and when I got there, I was super calm. It was dark weather, and everyone was nervous. I knew I just had to do everything the same. I skied all in, took the risk, and it went well. I now know that I can perform in any different situation, and this gives me huge confidence as, at this point in my career, I know I can perform and win.

”

YORK'S NOTES

Something that Marco kept repeating was that finding the right routine can bring him comfort and help him perform when it matters, even in the most difficult and stressful situations. As he describes it, anything can happen beforehand – like the weather changing or finding yourself needing to take an impromptu midday nap – but in those last 10 minutes before a race, his routine prepares him and helps him unlock the right mindset and the right performance. He describes his use of visualisation nicely as well. Visualisation is his anchor, his routine, as he does it before every race. It's a skill he uses to predict the things that could happen during the race, and it gives him the flexibility to adapt to any situation.

BIONIC
ORTEMA
swissskiteam

LIAM LAWSON

GROWING UP IN NEW ZEALAND, LIAM LAWSON WAS FREQUENTLY TOLD IT WOULD BE IMPOSSIBLE FOR HIM TO BREAK INTO THE ULTRA-COMPETITIVE WORLD OF FORMULA 1. HE DIDN'T LISTEN.

A promising youngster, Liam signed with the Red Bull Junior Team in 2019 and went on to pick up race victories in various championships all around the world.

He made his F1 debut in 2023 for the team that was then named Scuderia AlphaTauri and impressed during his five-race stint as the replacement for an injured Daniel Ricciardo.

It was the culmination of a lifetime's dedication and preparation needed to race at the pinnacle of motorsport – and his progress has not stopped there. After starting 2024 as a reserve driver, he was chosen to race the final six rounds of the season for Visa Cash App RB (formerly Scuderia AlphaTauri), and he was further rewarded for his promising performances with an Oracle Red Bull Racing seat for 2025 alongside Max Verstappen.

" —

Being a reserve driver is an amazing opportunity. The role consists of basically doing everything a driver does except actually driving the car at the track. Away from the track, it's mainly development work. The main drivers won't have as much time as we will to spend in the simulator and develop the car, so the team use the reserves to do a lot more hours in the simulator behind the scenes.

At the track, I'll attend all the debriefs and meetings. In the race, I'll have a headset on and listen to all the communication and experience everything that happens. The race weekends are a learning opportunity for us, as F1 is very different to any other racing championship, and it takes time to adjust.

— "

> *THE ULTIMATE GOAL IS TO WIN AND BE THE BEST. AS A DRIVER, I DIDN'T WORK THIS HARD FOR THIS LONG TO JUST DRIVE IN F1.*

S3, EP 2

LISTEN TO THE PODCAST HERE:

This meticulous approach meant that when a seat unexpectedly did become available at the Dutch Grand Prix in 2023, Lawson had the confidence to grab the opportunity with both hands, even though the odds were stacked against him.

"

As a driver, you have the self-confidence that you're good enough, but you never really know until you drive the car. When the call came, it was a bit stressful as I had just flown in from Japan and I knew those five races were a test of my future.

I felt a lot of emotion and a lot of pressure, but I worked with my driving coach Enzo Mucci, and I spoke to him a lot that day.

I had the self-belief and knew I was ready for Formula 1 but in this specific situation I was going to have one practice session on one of the hardest tracks on the calendar – and I knew the whole weekend was going to be wet.

No matter how ready you feel, when you're jumping in mid-season in a crazy situation like that, you can only be so ready, as I'd never driven the car before and I didn't have much time.

Now I've done it and experienced all of it, I know that I'm ready to race in Formula 1.

The ultimate goal is to win and be the best. As a driver, I didn't work this hard for this long to just drive in F1. I wouldn't be completely satisfied with that; the goal has been to win in F1.

"

YORK'S NOTES

At some point, everyone will likely experience similar feelings to Liam, of having to wait in the wings for an opportunity. Maybe there's a special project team at work you'd really like to be part of? Or perhaps you're more often on the subs' bench than among the starters for your sports team? Whatever the specific circumstances, we can all learn from Liam's commitment to doing everything it took to be ready. Liam used his time in the wings to learn from the other drivers, the mechanics, engineers, and everyone else to continue his development. When the opportunity finally came, he knew he'd done everything possible in terms of preparation, and so was ready to grab the opportunity with both hands.

YORK'S EXERCISE

PRE-PERFORMANCE ROUTINES SHOULD BE SEEN AS A ***GUIDING STRUCTURE*** OR ***FRAMEWORK*** THAT WE CAN USE TO ***ANCHOR OURSELVES.***

They shouldn't be perceived as rituals that have to happen in a specific way. Therefore, this exercise is all about developing a routine that focuses on the things we can control before a task or performance and removing focus away from the things we can't (see Chapter 8).

It's important to remember that some things are **fully in our control** and others are **fully out of our control,** but there is a lot **in between,** where we can have some level of **influence.**

It's helpful, then, to think about **three** categories in your preparation: the **controllable,** the **influenceable,** and the **uncontrollable.**

When approaching your planning for something important, you can **structure** your preparation according to these categories by **creating a list** of things that go in **each.**

4

Will the sound work on your presentation? That's **controllable** – if you get to the meeting **early** and do your technical check of the videos **in advance.** Will the power completely cut off and spoil your pitch? There's not much you can **do** about that! Will the audience **respond** in the way you **hope?** That's not something you can control, but you can **influence** the outcome by putting in the **work** and **practising** again and again.

5

If faced with something like that **power cut,** where it **really** is out of your control, **patience** plays an important role. In that kind of situation, where perhaps you're waiting for a technician to come and help, think about how you can **use the time well.** How will you **avoid** becoming frustrated while waiting? For more on that, read Konstanze Klosterhalfen's interview in the next chapter!

Q&A KAI TRAEMANN

Kai Traemann is a mental coach from Germany with decades of experience working at the highest level in sports and the media. He's also a passionate believer in the power of visualisation.

Throughout this book, multiple athletes refer to visualisation as a technique they frequently use in their quest to reach peak performance. Whether it's Marco Odermatt skiing a perfect run in his mind, Marcus Kleveland picturing landing a complex snowboard trick, or Karsten Warholm holding a clear picture of when and where he wants to peak on the track, visualisation can clearly be used to add focus, motivation, and confidence to succeed.

Most of us will have experience of visualisation in some form or another, whether consciously doing it or not! So, to explore this widely used tool further, we caught up with Kai, who has become convinced that visualisation is one of the most effective techniques in helping us reach our goals.

When did your mental coaching journey begin?

I started working with a mental coach myself around 14 years ago. I fell in love with it because, for me, it's one of the most valuable things you can learn in life. It's an amazing opportunity to get to know yourself better and discover how to handle challenges and problems in a way that works for you and your surroundings. The key is being able to control your state of mind whenever you need to. This is important not only for athletes but also for anyone going about their daily life.

> ”
> *THE KEY IS BEING ABLE TO CONTROL YOUR STATE OF MIND WHENEVER YOU NEED TO. THIS IS IMPORTANT NOT ONLY FOR ATHLETES BUT ALSO FOR ANYONE GOING ABOUT THEIR DAILY LIFE.*

What mental techniques do you find the most effective in your role as a mental coach?

I think visualisation is one of the most helpful techniques. It allows you to feel like you've already reached your goal. Let's say a footballer visualises the ball and their movements before a match. So, a week, a day, or even just an hour before the game, they'll start imagining the entire match during training. They visualise what it looks like, what it feels like, to be in their best form and achieve their goal. This can be incredibly powerful.

> ”
> *THEY VISUALISE WHAT IT LOOKS LIKE, WHAT IT FEELS LIKE, TO BE IN THEIR BEST FORM AND ACHIEVE THEIR GOAL. THIS CAN BE INCREDIBLY POWERFUL.*

Do you incorporate visualisation into your own routines as well?

Absolutely! Once, I had surgery on my throat, and the doctor warned me that it would be painful. I love the Caribbean and often go to St Lucia with my wife, so I decided to mentally take myself there during the surgery. I used all five senses to imagine it – seeing the water and beach, feeling the breeze, smelling the ocean, tasting the salty air, and hearing the waves.

This helped me stay calm, and afterwards the doctor told me he'd never experienced anything like it. Now we're talking about me helping him with patients who feel anxious before surgery, guiding them through the same process.

JUST STARTING WITH A POSITIVE THOUGHT CAN CHANGE YOUR MINDSET, AND EVERYTHING ELSE WILL FOLLOW.

Can you visualise anything, to help get you in a better frame of mind?

Yes, even something as simple as visualising your favourite cup of coffee can help. Even if you're in a bad mood! Think about its taste, smell, and how the cup feels in your hands. Just starting with a positive thought can change your mindset, and everything else will follow.

MAKE SURE YOU'RE CLEAR ABOUT WHAT'S IMPORTANT TO YOU, WHAT YOUR LIFE GOALS ARE, AND HOW YOU WANT TO MAKE A POSITIVE IMPACT ON YOURSELF AND OTHERS.

Do you have any tips on how people can start visualising?

A good starting point is to create a vision board in your bedroom. Print out pictures or write down words that represent your goals and stick them on the wall. When you go to bed, it's the last thing you see, and when you wake up, it's the first thing you look at.

This is a simple but effective way to feed your mind positive thoughts before you sleep and after you wake up. It's like setting your mental GPS for the day. All you need is some paper, a wall, and your imagination. It's an easy way to start visualising before moving on to more advanced techniques.

THE KEY IS THAT YOU REALLY WANT IT AND CAN FULLY IMMERSE YOURSELF IN THE EXPERIENCE USING ALL FIVE SENSES.

What are some important factors to remember before starting your visualisation journey?

The most important thing is knowing who you are and what your values are. Make sure you're clear about what's important to you, what your life goals are, and how you want to make a positive impact on yourself and others. Once you know that, visualisation becomes much easier.

It doesn't matter whether you're aiming to become a professional athlete, build a home with your family, or start your own company. The key is that you really want it and can fully immerse yourself in the experience using all five senses.

It's like setting a destination on your car's GPS – you know where you want to go and how you're going to get there, because you've already imagined the journey.

CHAPTER 6

BEING GOOD TO YOURSELF

INTRODUCTION

WHEN WAS THE LAST TIME YOU PRESSED PAUSE IN THE MIDDLE OF A BUSY DAY AND TOOK A MOMENT, HOWEVER SHORT, TO GIVE YOURSELF A MENTAL BREAK – TO CLOSE YOUR EYES FOR A COUPLE OF MINUTES, OR PRACTISE SOME YOGA OR MEDITATION?

IN THIS CHAPTER WE'LL LOOK AT:

Avoiding mental overload

Practising meditation

Staying patient

WE'LL HEAR FROM:

Pascal Siakam
"We're so consumed by the game every day. We eat and sleep basketball, so it's important to get away from it, relax, take your mind off the game, and find the balance."

Fernanda Maciel
"I learned the Vipassana technique, where the first thing you learn is how to observe your thoughts. I then transferred this knowledge to running."

Konstanze Klosterhalfen
"When I just wait and relax behind the leaders and wait for my moment, it always ends in a good result. At that moment, you think, 'OK, now it's your time.'"

In the hustle of day-to-day life, remembering to be good to ourselves has never been more important. Even making space for a few seconds to allow our brains to unwind, rest, and recover can make a big difference to our levels of satisfaction and productivity.

Switching off is often something that gets overlooked, perhaps because it seems to go against the grain of modern life. More and more, we seem to expect things to happen instantly, at the push of a button or the slightest of hand gestures. With digital devices at our fingertips providing us with noise, information, and instant access to every aspect of our life, it's easy to see how our brains can become overloaded with information.

When bidding to achieve our goals, it's common to be in constant pursuit of progress or results, to focus solely on becoming faster, stronger, fitter, and more successful.

During this chapter, we'll look at the importance of adding restful activities to the daily routine. We're going to explore how being good to ourselves and connecting with our mind and body can put us in a better position to avoid mental burnout and achieve success over an extended period.

Many elite athletes understand the advantages they can gain from focusing on mental recovery alongside their physical work. Let's look at a few examples.

> WHEN YOU COME INTO THE NBA AS A YOUNG GUY, IT'S REALLY TAXING NOT ONLY ON YOUR BODY BUT ALSO ON YOUR MIND. YOU HAVE TO BE ABLE TO TAKE CARE OF YOURSELF.

S2, EP 10

LISTEN TO THE PODCAST HERE:

PASCAL SIAKAM

POWER FORWARD PASCAL SIAKAM IS A TWO-TIME NBA ALL-STAR WHO'S ACHIEVED IT ALL ON THE BASKETBALL COURT.

The Cameroonian helped the Toronto Raptors clinch the Championship in 2019, and his consistent excellence across the relentless season has earned him a formidable reputation.

As Pascal explains, travelling city to city, playing game upon game, night after night, with millions watching around the world can be really taxing on the mind as well as the body. He understands that being in optimal condition involves more than just intense physical training and shooting drills. It requires a strict commitment to taking a step back, resting, and completely switching off. Only by avoiding mental overload and burnout can he perform to the best of his ability every time he takes the floor with his current team, the Indiana Pacers.

"—

Being in the NBA Finals in 2019, I don't think there's words to explain it. Being on that stage, and to be rewarded with the championship, was amazing. To see the joy we brought not only to ourselves and our families, but to the whole country in Canada – it's something I'll never forget.

The NBA can be super tough, though. The travel from different cities takes so much out of you, not only physically, but it's mentally draining as well. When you come into the NBA as a young guy, it's really taxing not only on your body but also your mind. You have to be able to take care of yourself and your body through things like rest and hydration, as it's such a long season with a lot of games and different cities every single day. You have to do the right things and have the right team around you to make sure your mind and body are right.

There're times when I take five to seven days off, where I just don't do anything. You need to relax, take your mind off the game, and just kick your feet up. At the end of the day, you're playing basketball with the best players in the world, but you have to be able to enjoy it. So it's important for the mind

and body to be able to rest and have some time for yourself.

In basketball, your body is everything, and the running and jumping is a lot for your body. A lot of athletes don't have longevity. If you don't do the right things to take care of yourself, it's impossible to do it for long periods. Recovery and nutrition are so important, so I focus a lot on that as an athlete.

There are so many things that can help you be durable and have a long career, in whatever it is that you do. The mental aspect and sports psychology is definitely one of them, and having people to talk to about what we're experiencing.

Sometimes I just want to talk about anything other than basketball with my family, and that's OK as well. It's also really important to have those people around you.

We're so consumed by the game every day. We eat and sleep basketball, so it's important to get away from it, relax, take your mind off the game, and find the balance.

YORK'S NOTES

Pascal is clearly so in tune with his mind and body. Not only does he pick up on the fact that he needs a break, but he also follows through with action. He understands what activities will allow him to mentally rest, and how beneficial they will be for him. This idea of mental recovery is an emerging field. It applies to high-level sport as well as our daily lives. Research is still ongoing into the impact that prolonged periods of high mental load can have on our bodies. Not taking mental breaks can lead to a burnout, so this is a really important topic.

See the exercise at the end of the chapter for some more thoughts on activities that are high and low frequency for our brains.

Red Bull

FERNANDA MACIEL

SINCE INCORPORATING MEDITATION INTO HER TRAINING ROUTINE, FERNANDA MACIEL HAS BECOME ONE OF THE MOST RENOWNED ENDURANCE ATHLETES IN THE WORLD.

The Brazilian ultrarunner started learning the Vipassana technique in 2006 and has since experienced benefits such as forging a stronger connection with her body and being able to automatically filter between her negative and positive emotions.

In the following extract, Fernanda explains how meditation helped her complete many challenges over gruelling distances and terrain, including ascending Gran Paradiso and the Matterhorn in the space of 24 hours, becoming the first woman to run up and down Argentina's 6,962-metre-high Aconcagua and conquering Antarctica's highest peak in record time.

"

I started to practise meditation a long time ago, in 2006. I learned the Vipassana technique, where the first thing you learn is how to observe your thoughts. I then transferred this knowledge to running.

The two techniques you learn are firstly to focus on your breathing, and then to focus on your body from the top of your head to your toes. You observe your thoughts, and you have the power to see how your heart is bumping and how your lungs are working.

When you close your eyes and start to observe your thoughts, you start to analyse all the things you were thinking about in the past, in the future, and all the things that can become worries.

When you are so deeply in this kind of meditation, you really know yourself inside. So, if you can filter these emotions and just focus on the positive thoughts, especially when running as you have so much time to think, that for sure is the best way.

It's like another form of training. Just like when you're training to do more and more kilometres and to run faster and faster, we can also train to think positively and not leave the negative thoughts to control you.

Doing this meditation helped me to better understand my body, especially to know when you feel good, when you feel bad, and when you've experienced certain emotions.

When we feel these amazing moments that are flowing with a run, it's good that we enjoy them to the maximum. When I have bad moments, like suffering with knee problems or stomach issues, it helps you keep moving because you know your path and you just need to keep moving.

A good example was my first high mountain, the Aconcagua in Argentina. At 6,962 metres, it's the highest mountain in the Americas. I became the first woman to run up and down this mountain in 22 hours.

I was around the mountain for two years and saw many professional ultrarunners trying. I achieved it on my third attempt. The first time, I got sick, I started to cough so much it could have damaged my lungs, so I had to go down. The second time I spent all night crossing rivers and after I reached base camp, I started to get altitude sickness and had to come down again.

> MEDITATION HAS DEFINITELY HELPED ME BETTER UNDERSTAND MY BODY. THE FIRST THING I LEARNED WAS HOW TO OBSERVE MY THOUGHTS. I THEN TRANSFERRED THIS KNOWLEDGE TO RUNNING.

S2, EP 6

LISTEN TO THE PODCAST HERE:

My third attempt, after a lot of acclimatisation and training, was perfect for me. I really felt that all the meditation I'd done, all my prayers and lessons I'd had with this mountain, had been like a school for me.

I arrived up at the top and remember thinking, "I can't believe this, maybe it is possible!" On the way down, everything was smooth and was just happening. I was achieving this crazy challenge, running all this way, and I was completely alone with just a full moon for company.

”

YORK'S NOTES

The use of meditation to boost high performance may surprise some people, but it's clear how much it's helped Fernanda. For her, it isn't just sitting at the top of a mountain for two hours; it's a way of filtering out debilitating emotions and other distractions, and it's clearly a very powerful technique. Meditating while running also bursts the common perception that meditation can only take place sitting down cross-legged. You can also enjoy the benefits while doing things like exercise, vacuuming, or doing a puzzle, for example. For Fernanda, it ultimately helps her concentrate on her performance, so it's obviously a very powerful aid.

> *MY BEST RACES ARE WHEN I STAY FOCUSED AND PATIENT UNTIL THE END. WHEN I JUST RELAX AND WAIT FOR MY MOMENT – IT ALWAYS ENDS IN A GOOD RESULT.*

S1, EP 18

LISTEN TO THE PODCAST HERE:

KONSTANZE KLOSTERHALFEN

GERMANY'S KONSTANZE KLOSTERHALFEN IS A MIDDLE-DISTANCE RUNNER WHO REGULARLY COMPETES FOR TOP HONOURS ON THE TRACK.

As a holder of multiple national records, World Championship bronze, and European Championship gold, she is known for waiting for the right moment in a race to up her speed and break for the finish line.

Holding back, pacing herself, and making the right decision as to when to attack her rivals is a difficult tactic to execute as it requires qualities you don't automatically associate with a running race – patience and calmness.

Here, she explains how she's been able to develop these attributes over the course of her career and how doing so has contributed to many of her career-defining performances.

" —

The World Athletics Championships in London in 2017, where I did the 1,500-metre, is probably the worst race to watch back for me, as I still remember how it felt.

It was the biggest event of the year, I'd been running good times beforehand, and I really wanted to make the final at my first World Championships. We thought about a race plan, which was to go hard in the middle of the race. I started sprinting and had a gap of about 100 metres on a world-class field. Two-hundred metres later, though, I slowed down, got passed by almost every woman in the field, and I didn't make the final.

That was very tough, but also a very good lesson for me. I had to learn how to become more patient. Patience is something I've had to learn over the years, and something that I'm still learning. Even in training, I often go out too fast sometimes. You have to channel this energy. You can't get too excited. My best races are when I stay focused and patient until the end and don't think about the result in the race.

I began to start practising being more patient when I moved to America. Sometimes we would have pacers who'd help us keep the pace right and we'd have to stay behind them and relax. It's not always easy, especially when you feel good, and you just want to go ahead.

I remember in races where I've stayed behind the leaders for 100 to 150 metres until I was actually ready to go when the big moment came. My bronze medal in 2019 in Doha, my first big international success, is a good example of where I stayed patient for a long time.

I was telling myself in the race, “Not yet, not yet!”, and I waited for the right opportunity. It’s an easy slogan to repeat in your head. I stayed patient and it definitely helped.

When I just wait and relax behind the leaders and wait for my moment, it always ends in a good result. At that moment, you think, “OK, now it’s your time!”, and even though there are other women around you, you know you can keep up and compete with them.

It’s exciting but you’re in control, as you know you’re ready and that you belong there. It’s probably the best feeling in a race, when you know you’re ready to go, even if it’s super-fast.

”

YORK'S NOTES

Patience is probably not the quality we automatically think of when it comes to high performance, but it's so important, and it's something we all struggle with at times in our daily lives. After all, modern society doesn't exactly encourage us to be patient. We want instant results at the click of a button and immediate gratification. While this is convenient, it doesn't always lead to the best outcomes. Konstanze's story is a great reminder that achieving our goals takes time, calmness, and patience.

YORK'S EXERCISE

SO, WHAT ***SMALL STEPS*** CAN WE TAKE RIGHT NOW TO ***IMPROVE*** OUR ***MENTAL WELLBEING*** BY ***REDUCING*** HOW MUCH WE ***TRIGGER*** OUR BRAIN?
EVEN IF WE ONLY HAVE A COUPLE OF MINUTES TO SPARE IN THE DAY, HOW CAN WE ENSURE WE HAVE THE ***NECESSARY PATIENCE*** TO JUST ***TAKE A MOMENT*** AND BE WITH OUR ***OWN THOUGHTS?***

1

Firstly, we need to **understand the signals** your **body** can send if the **brain** is **overloaded.** They'll be different for everybody, but symptoms could be things like **changes** in sleeping patterns, waking up feeling unrested, or not finding enjoyment in daily activities like walking outside.

2

Secondly, learn what activities require **high-frequency beta brainwaves** that are strenuous on the brain and other activities that use lower-frequency alpha brainwaves, which **help** the brain **rest, recover, and recharge.**

Strenuous activities for the brain	**Relaxing activities for the brain**
Watching TV	Light exercise like walking
Scrolling on phone	Meditation
Responding to emails	Talking with a friend
	Listening to music
	Reading a book

3

Next, remember that an **effective mental break** can be as short as just **a few seconds.** As a simple exercise, close your eyes and **remain still** for 30 seconds. Maybe set a timer or an alarm to help you. Can you **resist** the urge to open your eyes? Did you want to look at your phone?

4

Now, get into a habit of **repeating** the previous step, **extending** the time on each occasion. Can you rest for a minute? Five minutes? Maybe even half an hour?

5

If you practise this **often and consistently,** it won't take you long to start noticing the **benefits** of taking mental breaks.

Q&A HAZAL NEHIR

Hazal Nehir is one of the world's best known free-runners, who made her film stunt debut in Hollywood director Michael Bay's film *6 Underground.*

Being a freerunner while managing a fear of heights has brought many challenges for Hazal – not least, the negative self-talk that used to fill her head before she was about to leap from building to building.

By learning to be kinder to herself and not as self-critical when things go wrong, the Turkish athlete has been able to better face her fears and find enjoyment in her training and performances.

Here, Hazal reveals how remaining positive and logical in these times of high stress can be the difference-maker in achieving your ultimate goals.

What aspect of parkour, or freerunning, do you find most challenging, and how do you cope with it?

It really depends on what you're doing, but I generally struggle the most with high jumps, where there can be a 10-storey drop in between. You're literally on the edge of the roof, which is challenging for me because I'm scared of heights. When I train, sometimes I can't even stand on the edge or look down. At those moments, I realise how overwhelmed I am by the drop. Sometimes I need to step back, breathe, remind myself that everything is okay, and then return to the task and try again.

”

I ALSO WANT TO PUSH MYSELF PHYSICALLY AND MENTALLY, DISCOVERING HOW FAR I CAN GO.

What drives you to continue pursuing parkour, and what do you hope to achieve through it?

I think the most important thing for me is to inspire young girls and boys. I also want to push myself physically and mentally, discovering how far I can go. There's an unlimited potential in this, where you can always find yourself and experience joy. It's simply fun.

How do you stay motivated when facing what sound like pretty overwhelming challenges?

Yes, it can be overwhelming at times. If I focus on the end goal, it doesn't work for me, because I get overwhelmed and lose motivation. So I set small goals instead. I don't participate in tournaments or competitions; instead, I focus on finding specific jumps that I want to achieve. Sometimes, the jumps are intimidating, like a 10-storey height, so I work on smaller, less overwhelming jumps first, step by step. Eventually, I hope to reach my ultimate goal. I believe that we shouldn't focus solely on reaching the top of the mountain. We should focus on the next step, and that's how we can actually achieve our goals.

IT'S A CONSTANT MENTAL BATTLE, WITH ONE PART OF YOUR MIND SAYING YOU CAN DO IT AND ANOTHER SAYING YOU CAN'T. FINDING THE LOGICAL VOICE AMIDST THIS INNER DIALOGUE IS REALLY DIFFICULT AT TIMES.

Could you talk a little about your preparation, and the challenges of being up there on the rooftop?

Of course, we do a lot of training at ground level before attempting anything on rooftops. And yes, we do calculate the distances, and it helps to understand how much we can cover. But when you're on a roof, it's not always possible to measure precisely, so you have to trust your eyes. However, sometimes your eyes can deceive you. It's a constant mental battle, with one part of your mind saying you can do it and another saying you can't. Finding the logical voice amidst this inner dialogue is really difficult at times.

How has positive self-talk impacted your approach?

For me, positive self-talk is essential. I used to be very self-critical, telling myself that I was bad at a particular jump or questioning the point of all my training. But I learned to be kinder to myself, understanding that it's OK not to succeed immediately. There will always be challenges I can't conquer right away, and in those moments, it's important to stay positive and logical, recognising that while I may not succeed today, I can always try again tomorrow.

Do you believe it's more important to work on your weaknesses or to focus on your strengths?

While it's important to work on your weaknesses, I find the most joy in doing things I'm good at. I seek out challenges that bring me the most happiness and focus on those.

Do you put a lot of pressure on yourself?

I don't think I put too much pressure on myself outside of parkour. The sport itself can be demanding, and I admit that I'm a bit of a perfectionist, which doesn't help. But I'm learning to be kinder to myself and not to strive for perfection all the time.

How do you balance having a clear purpose with the need for adaptability in your journey?

I think it's important to have a purpose, but it's equally important to be adaptable because your purpose can change. It's not just black and white; there are many shades and colours in between.

What do you think makes parkour different compared to other sports, and how does it challenge both your mind and body?

Parkour is such a unique sport because it allows you to do whatever you want. It offers freedom in both mental and physical experiences.

When you face a challenge, it's about understanding why you're scared or why you think you can or can't do something. It's all about questioning and understanding, especially when there's a physical consequence in front of you. You can't just attempt it without first understanding what's going on in your mind.

How has your approach evolved since you first started?

When I first started parkour, it was just for fun, training with friends and enjoying the environment. But as I got deeper into it, I realised it can be really challenging. You need to figure out what you want to do with the sport and then pursue it with a solid plan that's still adaptable. Parkour teaches you this because there are so many uncontrollable elements when training outdoors, like the weather or being asked to leave a location. You have to stay adaptable.

How did your approach to training change after your injury, and what lessons did you learn from that experience?

After my injury, I learned to listen to my mind. If something doesn't feel right, I don't force it. I let it go and return to it later, without stress or expectations. I just try to have fun while still pushing myself.

LEIF OLAV ALNES

INSIDE THE SPECIAL RELATIONSHIP BETWEEN COACH AND ATHLETE

Leif Olav Alnes is a sports scientist specialising in biomechanics and a trusted coach, whose methods have helped Karsten Warholm become a world record-holder and Olympic champion in Tokyo in the 400-metre hurdles.

Karsten's bond with Leif Olav Alnes goes beyond that of a standard athlete-and-coach relationship. Coach Leif is a friend, mentor, and sounding board all rolled into one.

They're so committed to finding perfection that it's not uncommon for them to communicate for up to 12 hours a day.

Coach Leif's methods and techniques have pushed Karsten to become a world record-holder and Olympic champion in the 400-metre hurdles.

Describing himself as rational and optimistic, Leif's detail-oriented approach leaves no stone unturned in developing success for his athletes. And, as he reveals, communication and journaling are at the core of his daily tasks.

How do you approach your role as a coach?

I think that you are, in many ways, a mentor, and it's a big responsibility, and you shouldn't abuse that power.

As a coach, what's your biggest strength?

I'd rather let others speak on that, but I think I'm very optimistic. I think I'm reality based. I think I'm pretty rational, and I don't lose it.

Is developing mental strength key to success?

It's not quite that simple but I think mental strength will help you to achieve your best results when it matters. I think it increases the chance of you performing at the right time, because it's tougher to perform when the pressure is on.

WHEN THE LIGHTS ARE OFF, WHAT KIND OF PERSON DO YOU WANT TO BE? NOT WHAT YOU WANT TO TELL THE OTHERS YOU ARE, BUT WHO DO YOU REALLY WANT TO BE?

What does an athlete need in order to achieve their peak performance?

I say there are three things you need to do to have success. One, you have to be fit. And by fitness, I mean well-trained fitness; you have to train a long time before the competition. Then you have to be fresh. And freshness is also a long-term thing, but getting near the competition, it's easy to destroy the freshness, because you are uncertain that you are at the right level. And the last one of the three is, don't muck it up! Fit, fresh, and don't muck it up! If you're able to do that, you will do your best performance.

What struck you about Karsten when you first started working with him?

You have 10 obstacles in hurdles and every time you reach one, there's a chance you'll make a mistake. I remember the first time I met the great (400m hurdles runner) Edwin Moses, he said: "There are 35 things that go wrong in the hurdles." Karsten was only 20, and he said, "Edwin, aren't there also 35 things that can go right?" And I thought: "Yes! This man we can work with."

What is his biggest asset?

I'm very honoured to work with him. He has a really good brain for competition, he understands what's important and what's less important, and he is willing to prioritise, because sport, or life in general, is about prioritising. And the thing is, you have to prioritise things you like, even things you really like, to achieve something you want even more.

How do you guide an athlete like Karsten?

I always want the athlete to have ownership. I want every person to be the star of their own life. The problems start when people want to be stars in other people's lives, and there are quite a few of those.

I think it's so important that you let the athlete make the decisions. You just try to explain the choices. Like when he won and set the world record in Tokyo (2021), I said, "Now you have three choices. You could quit because you won everything. Two, you could start chasing the money. Or three, if you like this life, you can keep your eye on the ball and keep pushing and see where it takes you." I explained the options and he made the choice.

What are some of the biggest challenges you face?

I think most of the challenges in the world are to control human nature. Every person has an animal inside of a certain size. That animal doesn't have to be nice, and very often it is not. And then you have who you want to be. I think the big battle is between your animal and who you want to be, and that's a great battle. When the lights are off, what kind of person do you want to be? Not what you want to tell the others you are, but who do you really want to be?

How do you prepare for success?

On Monday, Wednesday, and Friday we get in at 10am and we stay until 7pm. We call these the red days, when you live your life in the training. Tuesday, Thursday, and Saturday are shorter days, and Sunday we are mostly off. When the training is done, I go home, I eat dinner with my family, I go to the computer, and I log everything. I write a patient journal of everything that was done and then we speak on the phone later. We have a debrief. It's almost like a military operation. How did today go? And what are we going to do for tomorrow?

How much do you communicate on a daily basis?

A lot! Even on a Sunday, Karsten comes to my home, and we sit in a hot tub in my garden, and my wife is always wondering, how can you guys talk so long? Because the record is three hours 47 minutes or something, in 40-degree water! She can't understand how we can do that.

All these ongoing conversations that you have 12 hours a day – do you plan them? Or is it free-flow?

Our conversations are free-flow because I think what's on your mind is more interesting. If it was to plan, you could write a letter or write something down. When you go to a meeting where everything is decided, I say, "If it's already decided, why do you need a meeting? You can just give out the instructions."

So I think, in any relationship, with your dog or your partner or whatever, the two things that are really, really important are mutual respect and communication. And communication should go both ways. If you feel that we are always looking for the best solution, two brains are better than one.

You mentioned about journaling; what do you take from this?

Nobody sees it, but I do it. It is very strong and very secure, because I think it's patient information – I don't even show it to the athlete. I write, I try to be unbelievably honest, scarily honest, about what I think and if something is good or bad.

Karsten roars, pounds his chest, and slaps his legs before a run. Is that something that you tell him to do? Could you explain if there is a mental aspect behind this?

You have to psych yourself up, so you try to prepare yourself. He even rips clothes in training! You see, there's a lot of rituals, so it's kind of trying to get to a situation where the pressure is on and you try to perform, and you get the adrenaline pumping. For him, it works. It's a way to get into the Viking warrior mode. It's not for the audience or anything. It's him trying to enter his war mode.

KARSTEN WARHOLM

Karsten Warholm is the fastest 400-metre hurdler in history and an athlete who lights up the track every time he competes.

Known for his speed and formidable mentality, Karsten is an unmissable presence on the start line with his pre-race routine of standing in the blocks roaring, beating his chest, and pounding his legs.

It's not just an act for the crowd, though – everything he does is meticulously planned in collaboration with his coach Leif Olav Alnes. Together, they have redefined how to approach the discipline of hurdling, through their detailed mental and physical preparation.

Confidence, communication, and visualisation are all key factors to Karsten's success, so we asked him to take us behind the scenes and explain further the techniques he uses daily to become such a dominant force.

How do you train your mental strength with Coach Leif?

Honestly, it's not that we always discuss these things in a structured way. It's more about building a good friendship and relationship where we just talk openly. I believe we have very good communication. We never let problems escalate; we always talk things through.

We analyse situations and discuss not how to win but how to find the best solution. It's not specific mental training, but the way we communicate in our everyday life involves a lot of mental preparation. We don't sit down for formal mental training, but our working relationship is mental training in itself.

I THINK A LOT OF IT COMES DOWN TO CONFIDENCE. YOU SHOULD NEVER CONFUSE CONFIDENCE WITH BEING COCKY OR ARROGANT.

How would you describe the feeling of being mentally strong?

I think a lot of it comes down to confidence. You should never confuse confidence with being cocky or arrogant. Confidence means genuinely believing that you can achieve something. When faced with a task, you know deep inside that you can accomplish it, that you can go out there and win, and perform. But you really need to believe it. You must have done all the right preparations, the right work, and have a good process that you trust. Confidence is the key.

Do you think being self-confident is your greatest mental strength?

Before confidence, I think the ability to put in the work, having the determination and passion to follow through, and executing the job with high quality every day is also crucial. In my sport, it's essential to do the physical part right, which comes with training. The results you see are because I've been able to train consistently over the last five, six, seven, eight years, avoiding serious injuries, doing the right things, and preparing correctly. The ability to train, prepare, and find the motivation to do it every day, even without 70,000 people watching, is equally important.

What do you do to create motivation, especially when you're tired?

For me, the biggest motivation is knowing that there will be major competitions in the future where I want to perform. In our sport, it's not enjoyable unless you're competing at the highest level. My main motivation is the knowledge that there will be important competitions, and I need to be prepared. If not, I'll lose, and that's something I really dislike.

You're known for roaring and hitting yourself in the build-up to races. Could you give us the thinking behind that?

For me, it started in training. The reason I began doing it was to find ways to get the adrenaline going, almost as if I were in a competition. I began doing it in training, and then it naturally carried over to competitions. It helps me switch on the fighting mode, getting into the zone where both your body and mind know that it's time to perform.

Is there another mental technique you use that helps you perform better?

In my everyday life, I think a lot about the moments when I want to be in peak condition and perform well. This helps me to maintain focus and make the right decisions. It's a form of visualisation, where you play through scenarios in your mind and keep them in your subconscious for when you train or compete.

Could you describe a moment in your career where your mental strength played a key role?

The first time I truly experienced this was in Tokyo in 2021. I knew I was in excellent shape, having broken the world record just before, and I knew this was probably my biggest chance to win a gold medal. There's a lot of pressure and tension in your body, but if you can control it, it can lead to a good performance. I remember the last 24 hours leading up to the race, thinking that this moment could define the rest of my professional career and life. Everything builds up in your body over those 24 hours. I was extremely focused that day, really in the zone and ready to attack the race. That's when I managed to put myself in the mental state needed to reach my full potential.

Do you revisit that moment in your mind?

Yes, sometimes I do. It helps me because when you experience something that makes you feel good, you want to achieve it again. You're always searching for that same feeling, and I use it for motivation, looking back and trying to recreate those moments whenever possible.

You are known for enjoying Lego. Does it also help you mentally relax?

Yes, I would say it started during the pandemic. It was something I did to relax and take my mind off everything – training, preparations, etc. It allowed me to get into my own zone where I didn't have to think about anything else. That's why I started doing it, to shut out the world for a little while.

What key lessons have you taken from Coach Leif?

First of all, his passion for what he does. You can see that if you're passionate about something and work hard to become the best at it, there's a good chance of success. But it's also about how he balances this with not always being overly serious. He focuses on enjoying the process and having fun, which I appreciate, because, in sport, if you want to succeed, you need to do it for a long time. To sustain that, you should enjoy yourself. It's important to look back and think, "We had a good time; it was fun." He's also very analytical, always looking at the facts and making decisions based on them, without letting emotions interfere.

Have you applied any of the mental techniques or lessons from your training to your daily life?

Yes, very much so. I've learned a lot from him, and because we spend so much time together, I naturally adopt these things. I try to live my life as I've learned from Leif: to have fun, not stress over things, but also do everything with excellence. If you're going to do something, do it right and do it well. I think it's a good way to live.

Would you say that making adjustments rather than radical changes has been a key factor in your success?

We always look for small improvements. I agree with my coach: when you have something that works – we still hold the world record and have the most gold medals – you shouldn't make drastic changes. You should focus on small improvements, as most of what we're doing is correct. If you change everything, it won't be successful because your body is trained to handle the stress you put on it every day. If you make changes, they should be incremental, not drastic, as the body needs to adapt gradually.

Coach Leif journals every training session. Do you do the same?

No, that's not my style. He's very analytical and invested in the process, but I'm not the type who writes everything down. I'm more relaxed. I believe sometimes striving for perfection can be counterproductive. If everything you do has to be of the highest quality, it can be stressful and burdensome. I think it's important to live in a way that feels relaxed and good inside. For me, writing everything down and maintaining strict control is too stressful. However, he likes having that control, so he does it, and in that sense, we complement each other well.

DR PETER SCHNEIDER

THE ROLE OF TEAM PSYCHOLOGIST

For someone with twin passions for psychology and soccer, working for one of the top teams in Europe is just about the perfect assignment, and for the last three years, Dr Peter Schneider has been living out his dream at RB Leipzig.

His role as Mental Performance Coach means working alongside exciting talent like Xavi Simons (see Chapter 2) and helping players develop the mental flexibility to thrive amid the high-pressure world of professional football.

Dr Schneider joined Xavi for the original interview, and here we highlight some of the insights he provided on topics like dealing with anxiety, planning, and staying in the moment.

HAVING A STRONG MINDSET IS MORE ABOUT BEING MENTALLY FLEXIBLE. JUST LIKE YOUR MUSCLES OR JOINTS, YOU WANT TO GET IN SUCH SHAPE THAT YOU CAN TAKE A GOOD HIT.

Can you explain what your job as a mental coach entails?

It's basically twofold. I work with the boys on individual things; for example, sleep is a big thing that we focus on. There's a lot of aspects around mental performance that we can look at: concentration or cognitive things, reaction, stuff like that.

And then as a general idea, I try to give the team good messages throughout the week and then for the weekend just to help them feel good mentally, feel confident – regardless whether we won or tied or lost – so that we have a nice stable environment, a good environment. I think it's probably the number one thing.

HAVING A STRONG MINDSET IS MORE ABOUT BEING MENTALLY FLEXIBLE. JUST LIKE YOUR MUSCLES OR JOINTS, YOU WANT TO GET IN SUCH SHAPE THAT YOU CAN TAKE A GOOD HIT.

What would you say makes a strong mindset?

Having a strong mindset is more about being mentally flexible. Just like your muscles or joints, you want to get in such shape that you can take a good hit. And it's not always about being tough. I think mental toughness is a phrase that people always like to use but at the highest level it's not really about being tough so much as being flexible. It's about dealing with consistent pressure, whether within a match or between matches. And one of the things I stress to the boys is they're allowed to have really negative emotions; they're allowed to be angry. And even if they want to say they feel weak or they don't feel great – that's fine. That's what a good mindset is, it's accepting that you're human and still performing.

There's a lot of pressure on the players you work with to perform well, and football fans tend to be armchair critics. Does the public nature of what you do make your job more difficult?

It's just one of those things. I'll give you an example. I might go see some friends and all they want to talk about is my job, and that's no problem. But then, of course, they are quick to judge and talk about people that I know on a personal basis. And I'll say, "You don't know anything about this person except the 90 minutes you see on the weekend." I see them every day, how much they care and how much they want to do something, you know? The classic line that drives me insane is, "Is he even training during the week? Does he even care?" I get so upset because, you know – that player had the mentality to get to where he is. And they're sitting on the couch watching him. Don't just judge based on the things you see, because there's so much more than just the 90 minutes you watch on the weekend. And that's something to be celebrated, in my opinion. One of my favourite things I like to do is figure out who they are besides footballers.

And it can affect the players, you know; reading angry comments on Instagram is not fun. But if I know that what's important to me is playing football and having fun and not reading comments, then I'm going to focus on playing football and having fun.

As simple as that sounds, that's the mental flexibility I'm talking about. It's knowing what's important to me. Is it really important to me what other people say?

Making it as a professional footballer is obviously incredibly difficult in such a competitive area. How do you suggest people deal with discouragement and rejection if or when they encounter it?

I've worked in academy football with younger players, and they'll be 15 or 16 years old and they'll have a coach that'll come along and say, "You're not good enough, you're not going to make it." That's crazy! They're 16 years old! That's a massively absolute statement to be making to someone who is so young, because, even at 16, you have so much time to grow.

But in my opinion, if someone comes to you and bluntly says, "I don't think you're good enough to make it" and you honestly do believe in yourself, then you've got to find a different way. If the good people around you are being honest, and saying, "We do believe in you", then it is on you to find another way. I think the silliest thing someone can do is say, "Well, this one coach, this one way, doesn't work, so I can't make it."

How do you help players manage their emotions before a big match or opportunity?

I say, "Just play football!", because when you play football, you feel good. And it sounds so simple, but let's say there's someone who's never been in a stadium – one of the myths that they believe is there's so much noise and things are so crazy that you're distracted. But in fact, you're just playing football and you're not even noticing most of the things, because you're just so into it. But maybe that kid, that first time he's on the pitch? Oh, he's noticing it! The reality is, the quicker you can get focused on playing football, the more you'll notice that the 20,000, 40,000 people in the crowd, they melt away real quick.

ANXIETY IS BASICALLY THINKING ABOUT AN OUTCOME THAT HASN'T HAPPENED YET.

What if players are experiencing performance anxiety – how do you help them?

Well, let's take it apart in a couple of situations. There's match performance anxiety – I don't know if I would call that anxiety. With penalties, there's definitely more anxiety. But the biggest reason for anxiety is because you have time to stop and think.

Anxiety is basically thinking about an outcome that hasn't happened yet. So when you're walking up to take a penalty, first of all you have the final aspect of it: it can end the match or a tournament, so there's this massive outcome looming.

But the second thing is, you have this walk from the midline, usually all the way to the penalty spot. And if you ask me, the best players know exactly what they're going to do from that line to the ball. They have a thought process, a routine. And then they probably have that flexibility that I'm talking about, so that if you have a goalie who wants to dance a little bit or throw the ball in the air, they're going to go, "Oh yeah, that can happen. No problem, I can deal with that; I have a plan for that." And that kind of pulls anxiety away. So, I think penalties – and specifically penalty shootouts – have their own kind of flavour.

But in a match, it's a little bit different. What I see on the pitch when we play a very talented team is not so much anxiety about the future, but more that you're just overloaded. You might be so overloaded that you don't see the right decision, you have too much tunnel vision, and you can't see the wider game. So, you can't make the relaxed pass and you can't shoot the ball with the right touch.

At RB Leipzig, you work with individuals like Xavi Simons. How do you think your role as a mental coach is distinct from the other coaches he works with?

I don't need to talk to Xavi so much about what he did on the weekend, because there are three or four other experts here that are going to say, "Hey, you need to open up quicker, you need to stand there, you need to shoot there", or, "You did everything 100% right." Athletic coaches are going to take care of them physically. One of the things I like to do is always enquire, "Hey, man, all good? You need anything?" I mean, a relationship like this depends on how open the player is willing to be. This is about trust; it's about connection as well.

And what about your role in building the team as a whole?

One thing I do, when we do team-building activities, is to have somebody captain the team who's a little quiet or maybe doesn't have as much responsibility, just to kind of get them to have more of a voice.

I think one of the advantages as the team psych or mental performance coach is that I have my eyes and ears open constantly. So I get to see who's fading a bit in the back; I notice them and give them the smallest amount of attention: "How are things going?" That's something I really appreciate being able to do, and I think the players notice as well. It is my job, but it doesn't feel like a job: it's a pleasure.

You've spoken about how important it is to be in the present to help you reach your goals. What advice would you give others about how best to stay focused on the present?

Honestly, two things: firstly, have good people around you that remind you of where you want to go. And then, for me, daily meditation or prayer gives me that connection back to myself and to what's important. I think meditation disconnects me from this steady stream of life, and especially with cell phones and so many things you can get caught up in really quickly. Turn off your mind, just listen to your own thoughts, and kind of ground yourself. Those things are essential, I think, for growth.

CHAPTER 7

STAYING AGILE

IN THIS CHAPTER WE'LL LOOK AT:

- **Building a growth mindset**
- **Recalibrating goals**
- **The art of not panicking**

WE'LL HEAR FROM:

- **Armand 'Mondo' Duplantis**
  "I hope that the fire and drive that I've had since I was three years old, and that I still have now, never goes away. I just hope I can do it for as long as I can and just keep pushing barriers."
- **Marc Márquez**
  "As an athlete, it's quite difficult to keep the same motivation for 20 races a year. So you must adapt and find some new tactics to keep you in that competitive mood."
- **Daniel Dhers**
  "One of the main things I always try to talk about now is being prepared for the unexpected. We have a lot of unexpected moments, especially in competition."

INTRODUCTION

GETTING STUCK IN OUR WAYS IS SOMETHING WE'RE ALL PRONE TO, ONE WAY OR ANOTHER. IF WE'RE PREPARED TO EMBRACE CHANGE, THOUGH, THERE ARE SOME POWERFUL AIDS TO IMPROVEMENT AVAILABLE TO US.

When you're used to doing something one way, and it's working pretty well, it's natural just to carry on, and of course sometimes that's the correct approach (see Chapter 5).

But the circumstances of life – at home, work, or wherever – are becoming less and less predictable, and few of us now would expect to live our lives without moving somewhere new, changing jobs, or taking on new challenges that are outside our comfort zone.

It may seem from the outside that high-performance athletes, especially in highly technical disciplines, are the masters of routine – that their main task is to perfect the art of doing the same thing over and over again, to the point where making mistakes is unthinkable. That's only half of the story, however, because great athletes are also highly adaptable in a variety of ways.

Yes, part of that is perpetually looking to improve in even quite small ways. You may have heard of the phrase "marginal gains", which boils down to the desire to make fine changes in any aspect of what you do to secure performance improvements that, while not much in themselves, can combine to make a significant difference.

But another key skill is the ability to take on board feedback, and being willing to change based on the observations of people you trust. And, crucially, great athletes know that sometimes you might have to change your goals if you're knocked off course – which of course goes hand in hand with resilience and bouncing back (see Chapter 10 for lots more on these topics). Here's how some of the best in global sport embrace the twin arts of seeking improvement and change.

ARMAND 'MONDO' DUPLANTIS

MONDO HAS TAKEN POLE VAULT TO HEIGHTS NEVER BEFORE SEEN IN HIS SPORT, SURPASSING THE PREVIOUS BENCHMARKS OF SERGEY BUBKA AND RENAUD LAVILLENIE IN HIS BID TO BECOME, UNQUESTIONABLY, THE GREATEST OF ALL TIME.

Mondo was born in Lafayette, Louisiana, to an American father and a Swedish mother. Still in his early twenties, he has already won every title imaginable representing Sweden. He is an Olympic, world, European, and Diamond League champion and he keeps on eclipsing his own world record – which he even managed to do in the Olympic final in Paris in 2024, when he thrilled crowds by clearing a staggering 6.25 metres to cap yet another gold-medal performance.

But he wasn't always someone brimming with confidence, and readily admits it was sport that helped him build a growth mindset that has buoyed his confidence levels both in training and competition and in everyday life. Here's what he had to say about goal setting.

"

Sports teaches you a lot of good lessons, and it definitely teaches you how important preparation is. You can't really expect anything to go well if you don't prepare for it, no matter what it is. You have to train your body and mind to do the things you want it to do.

You also have to know what you want to do and set goals to get there. They can be little goals like check marks to make sure that you're where you want to be. The only thing that matters is to be realistic with yourself, and sometimes it's just not the way the chips fall. But I think it's good to have big dreams and try to chase them because if you don't, there's no way you're going to know how far you can go.

You also need to follow your gut and follow what you really love and what you're passionate about. If you don't love something, and you're not passionate about what you're doing, it's going to be hard to improve and find yourself really happy in achieving your goals.

I'd like to be the best pole-vaulter that ever lived, and I think that's very possible for me. I hope that the fire and drive that I've had since I was three years old, and that I still have now, never goes away. I just hope I can do it for as long as I can and just keep pushing barriers.

It's literally just me and the bar; that's it, that's the game. I can't control what my competitors do. I'm just going to go out there and jump as high as I possibly can. So I'm more or less fighting against my personal best and it's more or less been like that since I was just starting out. It was my oldest brother who helped mould me into the man that I am today. For me, sport is what really made me a confident person. Growing up, I was insecure in normal kid ways. When I was able to get home and dive into pole vault, that felt like the most me that I can be. I was able to find myself within that, and I was able to be so free. It helped translate to other things. Now I consider myself a confident guy.

Back then, I'd always dream of one day being the world record-holder. For me, that first world record was pretty much a game changer. You become really grateful and really appreciative of the journey. I definitely gained this new level of self-confidence.

> *I'D LIKE TO BE THE BEST POLE-VAULTER THAT EVER LIVED, AND I THINK THAT'S VERY POSSIBLE FOR ME.*

S1, EP 3

LISTEN TO THE PODCAST HERE:

I guess some people think, when you break the world record, you're going to have this feeling of, "What's next?" because you've done something that nobody's ever done in the world and what's the motivation at that point?

But for me it was almost like I felt that I'd done this incredible feat, and now I want to prove to myself I am worthy of being the best ever, and I want to show people that this is not a fluke, this is what I am, this is what I've been doing. I wanted to build upon that momentum and try to keep pushing the barriers, because I felt like this was just the beginning of things.

"

YORK'S NOTES

Most of us appreciate that you can't become truly great at something without dedicated training, but what is sometimes underestimated is the value of having a plan or a goal for every practice session along the way. Mondo's experience speaks to that. He clearly has incredible passion for what he does, but when he's training, he knows that even that is not enough.

A good example here would be playing a musical instrument. Once you get to a certain level, you might find yourself sitting down at the piano, or picking up the guitar, and tinkering away at the same handful of pieces or songs. As you play them more and more often, there will probably come a point when you find that you've reached a plateau – you're not really getting much better, and you may even find that your enjoyment is waning.

One way to counteract this effect is to do what Mondo does and set a goal for yourself every single time you play. Maybe it's to make a first attempt at a new piece, or to only play a tricky section until you've got it down perfectly. Even setting small goals like this can make a big difference – in music, in sport, in whatever it is you want to get great at. This small goal doesn't even have to be directly related to becoming better at the task: you can get really creative with it. Maybe try playing the same song on the piano while saying the months of the year backwards! Or can you play the song on the guitar and jog on the spot?

> IN THE PAST I WAS ALWAYS THINKING ABOUT THE BIGGEST POSSIBLE THINGS, BUT YOU FORGET THAT IN ORDER TO ACHIEVE THIS BIG THING, YOU NEED TO ACHIEVE LOTS OF SMALLER THINGS.

S1, EP 25

LISTEN TO THE PODCAST HERE:

MARC MÁRQUEZ

SPAIN'S MARC MÁRQUEZ BECAME THE YOUNGEST MOTOGP™ CHAMPION IN HISTORY WHEN HE CLINCHED THE TITLE IN HIS DEBUT SEASON.

Five further championship wins in the premier class of the sport quickly followed as Marc established himself as the dominant force of his era.

But a nasty crash at the opening race of the 2020 season ended with him breaking his humerus. The comeback trail was a slow and painful process at first, and he underwent several different surgeries before he was able to challenge for race wins – which, thankfully, he is now again doing regularly.

Key for Marc was being able to reassess what his race-to-race goals were, as he explains here.

" —

I was winning nearly every year, and for me that became normal. Then one day, I was doing one of the best races of my life, and I crashed. I had a big injury and all of the nightmares started.

In 2020, 2021, and 2022, there were three years where I had four different surgeries on my arm. To keep the same motivation was impossible, but I was able to keep a positive mentality and to focus on my routines.

During that big injury, there were two different periods in my mentality. The first one was, "I will come back, and I will win!" But then I started to realise that something was not working in my body.

That is when the second part arrived. My expectations were high, but I realised that my arm was not ready to win races. This is when I started to put in some realistic goals, something that I could achieve.

Maybe it was a top 10, maybe it was a fifth position, maybe it was sixth position – it was not victory, but it was a target to keep me motivated.

I tried to find a realistic goal to achieve that would bring an extra boost to my body and help it continue.

If you're putting your target like, "I want to be world champion", then if you're not ready, it will only bring frustration, and then the motivation is going down and down and down.

In the past, I was always thinking about the biggest possible things, but you forget that in order to achieve this one big thing, you need to achieve lots of smaller things. When I was in a difficult moment, I said, "OK, I must change something." I needed to understand a way to find a small target to help me arrive at the biggest target one day.

As an athlete, it's quite difficult to keep the same motivation for 20 races a year. So you must adapt and find some new tactics to keep you in that competitive mood for training and races. You can't think about racing, racing, racing 24 hours a day – it's important to have your free time to relax.

"

YORK'S NOTES

It can be hard when you're used to winning everything in sight, to then find yourself in the situation where you can't realistically challenge for the top and have to change your expectations. Marc's attitude to that change in circumstances was a determination to continue setting goals, even if they wouldn't have been what he wanted in previous seasons. Instead of just saying, "OK, I can't win this race, so it doesn't really matter what I do", he insisted on having some kind of target that was within his reach. Having this kind of discipline can be really helpful psychologically, and not just in highly competitive arenas like professional sport. And don't forget, the most rewarding goal can also just be: "Today, I want to enjoy myself and not have any expectations or targets."

SHOEI
GIVES YOU WINGS
VERTICAL
Antangin
YOU-ALL
Kapriol
93
Estrella Galicia
Unibat
Gigetta
FEDERAL OIL
BOLD RIDERS
wonderful indonesia

DANIEL DHERS

ONE OF THE MOST DECORATED AND RESPECTED BMX RIDERS IN HISTORY – AND A BENCHMARK FOR MANY OF THE TOP RIDERS EVEN TODAY – DANIEL DHERS SURPRISED MANY BY PICKING UP A SILVER MEDAL AT THE TOKYO OLYMPICS AT THE AGE OF 36.

His path to the podium was far from easy, however, as the Venezuelan's gameplan was initially derailed. Using all his experience from a lengthy and illustrious career, which has brought him five X Games gold medals, he conjured up his own plan B. Here, he tells the story of how he did it.

" —

In competition, someone will throw a banana peel, and I've lived this many times already. I'll be at an event, and think, "I'm going to win this", and then someone pulls a rabbit out of the hat, and they just catch you with your pants down.

It can throw you off, as you're distracted. I don't want to go and end up getting 30th place when I could have just gotten second, so you can't freak out like you just lost the event. Freaking out is never the answer.

I remember one of my managers would always tell me, "Mental strength is the key." One of the main things I always try to talk about now is being prepared for the unexpected. We have a lot of unexpected moments, especially in competition.

I always tell everyone around me, regardless of what we're doing, that the number one thing you can do is never panic. Panic will not help. Yes, you will feel emotional, you're going to be super stressed or angry or sad, but don't panic! Look at the moment, analyse it, and concentrate on what could be the first step to fixing it.

Every situation is different, but your worst enemy is not being prepared. The Olympics are such a different event from everything else that we do, and everything I did in my life prepared me for it.

On day one, I got there and found the park didn't work! My line was disintegrated so I had

IN COMPETITION, SOMEONE WILL THROW A BANANA PEEL. I'LL BE AT AN EVENT AND THINK, "I'M GOING TO WIN THIS", AND THEN SOMEONE PULLS A RABBIT OUT OF THE HAT.

S2, EP 5

LISTEN TO THE PODCAST HERE:

another banana peel right off the gate! I was freaking out. I had this line in my head and now I can't do it. Damn. I remember thinking, "OK, what am I going to do?" The first thing was to not panic, to go tomorrow to practise, focus on the one part that has given you trouble and see if you can dig through it. By the third day, I had the line back. It was about adjusting and adapting.

I was 36 years old, I was meant to retire the year before, but I stayed because it was the Olympic Games and I thought I could make it and medal. I knew it was going to be hard and I'd need a lot of focused attention and to adapt as I went.

There's no perfect, fool-proof plan, but if you put steps in place for every time you have an unexpected situation, you'll be able to come out of it with more success. I guess, to me, that's been the secret to being around for so long.

YORK'S NOTES

Things will never ever go 100 per cent according to plan, but, as Daniel showed, it's not about having the perfect solution right there to hand. It's more about *how* you react to the thing going wrong. Daniel could have reacted in that moment by just being really annoyed, but he stayed positive, calmed himself down, and used his inner voice to help him deal with that situation. It was only later that he was able to figure out a solution. It has a lot to do with being very self-reflective. He's almost his own coach in that moment, and he's deploying skills that he has learned over many, many years.

YORK'S EXERCISE

WE ALL KNOW THAT THINGS ***DON'T*** ALWAYS GO IN A ***STRAIGHT LINE*** AND THAT IT'S ***IMPOSSIBLE*** TO PLAN FOR ***EVERY*** EVENTUALITY.

We can't always work out in advance exactly what we're going to do in any given situation; not all of us will have a plan B – let alone plans C, D, E, F, and G as well! What we can do, though, is prepare ourselves mentally for how we'll react if – or perhaps more likely when – something happens to knock us off course.

1

A good tool is to think about this kind of contingency planning as a **traffic light system,** with **green, amber, and red lights**. So the next time you're planning for a situation where you want to give your **best,** but you can't possibly control every single variable, try thinking about your mental preparation in these **"traffic light" terms.**

Green:

This means everything is **going to plan,** with no major upsets. In this situation, you can concentrate on **giving your best.** With **luck,** you might even approach something like **flow state** (see Chapter 4). But, as we all know, life **doesn't** always go according to plan, so you also need to think about what you'll do when the **amber** light flashes.

Amber:

If something does go **a bit wrong** and you have to slightly **adjust,** how do you want to **react** to that situation? You **don't** need to have the perfect solution already worked out, but having a **basic idea** of how you'll react to setbacks can make all the **difference** in that key moment. Think about how you will make sure you **remain calm** – maybe taking some fresh air for five minutes will help?

Red:

If you're in a situation where everything's going **extremely wrong,** it's important to understand what can help you **get back** to a level of **comfort** and a state of mind that enables you to make a **rational** decision. Again, it's not about **instantly** having all the answers; it's about **reacting** in such a way that gives you the best **chance** of finding a **solution.** Maybe undertaking some deep **breathing exercises** brings you clarity? Will a phone call to a friend, the sound of a **familiar voice,** work to reassure you? Or will some **physical exercise** help reduce the anger and frustration?

You **don't** have to have **specific plans** for how to solve every situation that might come up – but you can make a plan for how you're going to **respond** if the green light turns to amber or red.

YOUR NOTES

CHAPTER 8

ACCEPTING MISTAKES

INTRODUCTION

FAILURE IS SOMETHING WE ALL HAVE TO FACE AT SOME POINT IN OUR LIVES.

IN THIS CHAPTER WE'LL LOOK AT:

Learning lessons from defeat

How to keep backing yourself

Pressing the reset button

WE'LL HEAR FROM:

Matteo Berrettini
"Even the best years I had, I won maybe three or four tournaments, and I entered 25. So you have to learn how to lose."

Mario Gómez
"Of course, when I couldn't score or I couldn't handle the pressure because of the expectations, I had some doubts."

Daniela Ryf
"It's about how you manage your inner voices, stay positive, and not let the devil come up and put you in a negative spirit."

Whether it's an exam that doesn't go as well as we'd hoped, not getting the job we interviewed for, or experiencing the frustration of trying to express ourselves in a new language, at one time or another we've all felt we haven't exactly knocked it out of the park.

If there's ever a technique that sounds simple to master but in reality is really difficult, it's being able to react to failure in a positive way. When emotions are at play and we're in the middle of a challenging situation, spinning into a negative mindset can be tough to avoid.

It can be easier to blame external factors beyond our control instead of taking a more analytical look at ourselves and what we've done. By undertaking an honest kind of self-reflection, it's possible to reframe the situation to work to our advantage, by pinpointing what we actually did well and, on the other hand, where we have room for growth.

Hiding from our losses and approaching them in a negative frame of mind not only risks impacting our ability to achieve our goals in the moment, but it can also affect our self-belief and performance levels over an extended period of time.

It's fair to say that professional athletes have to deal with failure more than most. It doesn't matter how successful you are, in sports there are always moments when you perform below your best, when you miss a simple chance in front of goal, or just get beaten fair and square.

In this chapter we'll learn first-hand about the techniques that elite athletes adopt when confronted with disappointment and failure. We'll uncover how they're able to embrace their losses rather than letting themselves be defined by them. Pick up some tips on how to review your own setbacks effectively and bounce back with renewed confidence and focus.

> *IT'S IMPORTANT TO TAKE THE POSITIVES FROM A LOSS. IF YOU DON'T KNOW HOW TO LOSE, IF YOU DON'T KNOW WHAT TO TAKE FROM IT, IT'S HARD TO GET BETTER.*

S1, EP 26

LISTEN TO THE PODCAST HERE:

MATTEO BERRETTINI

TO BE AN ELITE TENNIS PLAYER, YOU NEED TO LEARN HOW TO LOSE. THAT'S THE VIEW OF FORMER WIMBLEDON FINALIST AND MULTIPLE ATP TOUR WINNER MATTEO BERRETTINI, ONE OF THE HARDEST-HITTING PLAYERS IN THE SPORT.

The Italian explains that even when you're ranked among the world's elite, and are capable of beating any opponent, the likelihood is that you'll still lose in almost every tournament you enter. That's just the nature of a sport where you're playing so often against players with generally similar levels of talent, focus, and will to win.

What helps Matteo continue to be successful on the tour is how he's able to negotiate these big moments of disappointment and come back stronger time after time.

"

Tennis is a mentally tough sport; you have to be patient, as sometimes the results don't come straight away. You have to be ready to lose, as most weeks you're not going to win the tournament. You look at how many tournaments you play every year, and almost every week you lose.

Even the best years I had, I won maybe three or four tournaments, and I entered 25. So, you have to learn how to lose. Since a very young age, all my coaches used to tell me, "You lose, you win, you learn, you move on."

It's something that's really attached to tennis. Maybe some kids lose less than others, but in the end every kid is losing at every level. So, it's important to take the positives from a loss. It's easy to say but not easy to do, as there are so many emotions – the anger, the fear. It took me a while, and it still takes me a while sometimes but it's the only mindset if you want to be a professional tennis player.

If you don't know how to lose, if you don't know what to take from the loss, it's hard to get better. This way of thinking taught me so much in life as well. There are bad moments – moments that you wish never happened – but in the future, you can get better, and I always use the same energy I have in tennis to get better.

I always welcome the bad feelings, as I believe if you feel bad about something, it means you care about it. It takes time to process and digest, but it always gives me the energy to step into the gym or onto the court and get better.

I call it the "wall" philosophy, in that every day you try to put a brick in your wall, and it becomes stronger. Sometimes you lose some bricks, sometimes you add some, but you have to feel like every day was useful and you embrace what's happening. The more bricks you put in, the more stable it is. I learn something about myself like this. In sport, if I take the good out of a loss or a bad moment, I'll be ready in the future for when the same moment happens.

You can say the same about life. During bad moments, you can always lean back on your memory, look back on your wall and know which way to go.

"

YORK'S NOTES

There are so many valuable lessons in Matteo's words. Sometimes we win, sometimes we lose. It's just a fact of life that we're not going to make every shot that we take. How we frame these moments of disappointment is what helps us improve and develop as individuals. When something goes wrong, it's a natural human reaction to focus on the negatives. Emotions are high and our impulsive thoughts can often take control. Matteo is very honest about how he still sometimes finds it difficult to get into a positive mindset after losing a close match, but he's always able to find a way to see the defeat as instructive. What positives can I take? What went well? What can I do better next time? These are all positive questions that Matteo asks himself to ensure that he's ready for the next match.

MARIO GÓMEZ

ONE OF THE MOST RESPECTED FORWARDS IN EUROPEAN FOOTBALL, MARIO PLAYED FOR THE LIKES OF BAYERN MUNICH, BESIKTAS, AND THE GERMAN NATIONAL TEAM DURING HIS FANTASTIC CAREER.

A powerful player with pace, intelligence, and a rare coolness in front of goal, Mario gave you the sense he was going to score every time he stepped out onto the pitch, but the added pressure that comes with that kind of reputation wasn't always easy to handle.

Over the course of his career, Mario developed the confidence to know that even if he missed a big chance during a match, he could blank out all the noise and still always be ready for when the next opportunity materialised. It's a lesson that served him well.

"—

My career was not always heading towards the top. There were many ups and downs. At the beginning, everything went up like crazy. I had my first games, I scored, and I was everybody's darling. And then of course with the first difficulties, when I couldn't score or I couldn't handle the pressure because of the expectations, you have some doubts.

But every year, I always scored a lot of goals, so I had the natural feeling in me that the next chance would come. Even if you miss a chance, the next chance to score will be there and everything will be fine again.

My sporting life told me and showed me that after rain, there's always sunshine. I believe this totally so I could always manage the situations, even when it was super difficult, and the whole stadium were whistling at me. I knew that the next chance would be there and if I scored, the people would be back on my side.

I went to the European Championship in 2008 aged 22. We were under a lot of pressure in the third game against Austria. I got a nice pass from Miro Klose and had an empty goal, one metre in front of me. I tried to kick it into the empty goal but there was a little hole in the grass and the ball jumped up and I didn't hit it in the right way, and it went up to the sky.

MY SPORTING LIFE SHOWED ME THAT AFTER RAIN, THERE'S ALWAYS SUNSHINE. I COULD ALWAYS MANAGE THE SITUATION BECAUSE I KNEW THE NEXT CHANCE WOULD BE THERE.

S1, EP 7

LISTEN TO THE PODCAST HERE:

I was just shocked. I couldn't move any more. What was happening? Being 22, I couldn't handle this situation. From that moment on, my head was out of the tournament.

Then, whenever we had a national team game, the whole stadium was against me, even our own fans. I even changed my style of play to get everybody back on side, but it took me 14 to 15 months to realise that this isn't possible.

I just told myself, I don't care about what people are thinking any more. It was not a single moment; it took weeks and months to realise this and to start following my own way. Slowly, I came back on track, and I think in 2012 I had the best year in my career and scored more than 50 goals for Bayern Munich.

YORK'S NOTES

Mario developed a mode of self-belief that was robust enough to help him deal with the kind of criticism that would be hard for anyone to take. Putting yourself back in the spotlight again and again, knowing that the next miss is probably just around the corner, takes a lot of courage – especially when playing in front of tens of thousands of fans in the stadium, and millions more watching on TV!

It's a great reminder that when we're able to focus on our own capabilities, to blank out the noise, we can achieve our best results. By having full confidence in our approach and knowledge that the path to success we've chosen is the right one to follow, as Mario says, the sunshine and the next chance will always come.

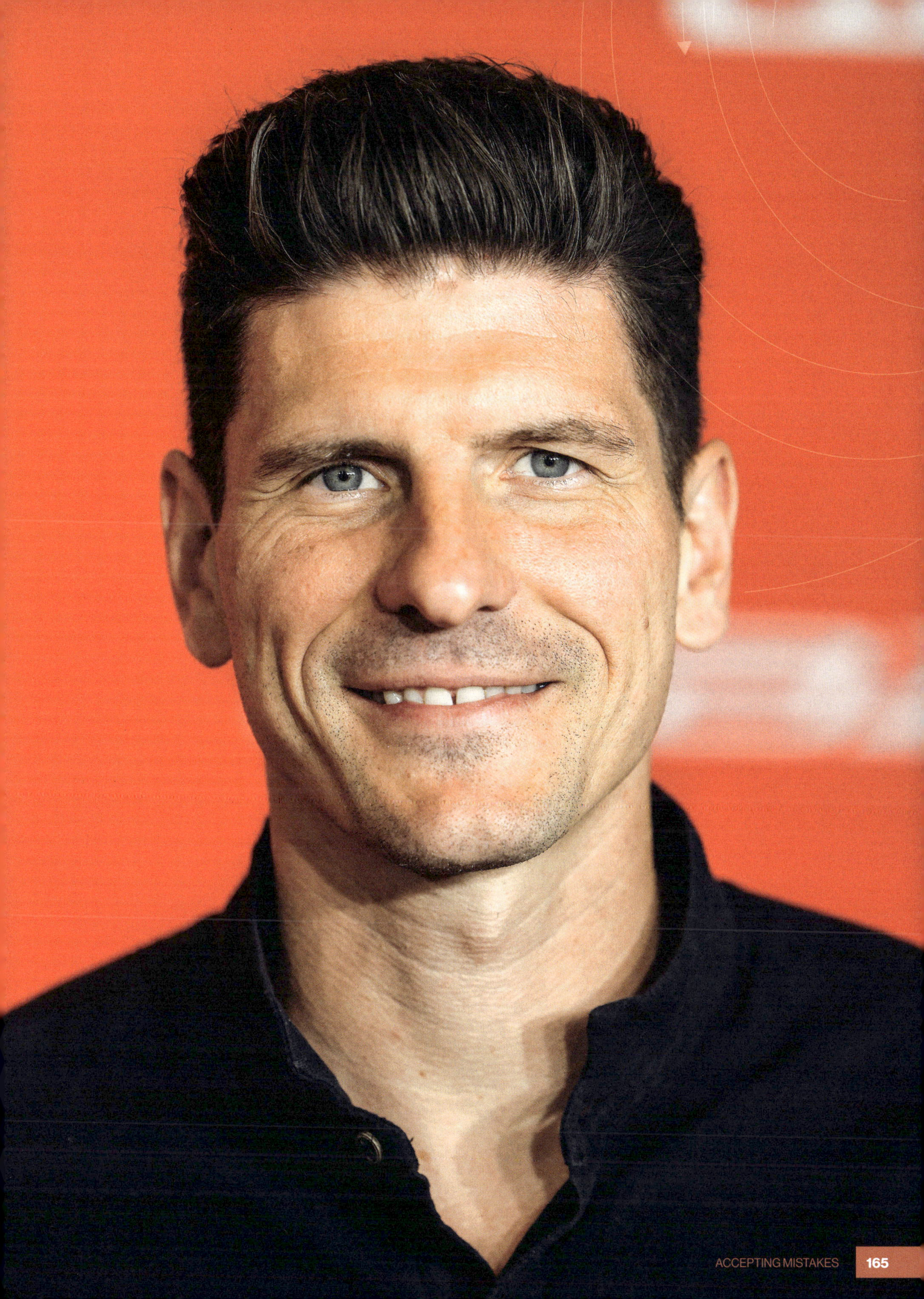

> ONE NEGATIVE THOUGHT CAN RUIN YOUR DAY, AND ONE POSITIVE THOUGHT CAN SAVE YOUR DAY. IT'S NOT ONLY TITLES THAT DEFINE SUCCESS; IT'S OVERCOMING CHALLENGES AND MAKING THE BEST OUT OF EVERY SITUATION.

S1, EP 16

LISTEN TO THE PODCAST HERE:

DANIELA RYF

WIDELY REGARDED AS ONE OF THE GREATEST IRONMAN ATHLETES OF ALL TIME, DANIELA IS A LEGENDARY COMPETITOR OVER A RACE THAT INVOLVES A 3.8-KILOMETRE SWIM AND 180 KILOMETRES ON THE BIKE FOLLOWED BY A FULL MARATHON OVER 42.2 KILOMETRES.

The Swiss triathlete's positive approach to overcoming setbacks and her ability to refocus quickly have been key to her five IRONMAN World Championship victories, four of which came consecutively between 2015 and 2018.

Fierce competition from rivals, injuries, mechanical failures, and even a jellyfish sting all threatened to derail Daniela's pursuit of greatness but each time she was hit by a setback or had a bad result in one of the disciplines, she was able to recover quickly rather than dwell on what had gone before.

“

In IRONMAN racing you spend a lot of time on your own and you can have bad moments. It's really about putting yourself in a positive spirit, and you need a lot of mental strength to dial in your thoughts, as your mind is responsible for how the body reacts.

It's about how you manage your inner voices, stay positive, and not let the devil come up and put you in a negative spirit.

In 2018 I was stung by a jellyfish just a few moments before the start. I didn't let the negative thoughts come up. In the swim it hurt a lot, and I was a little bit scared. I had a clear moment where I thought I couldn't finish the swim. I had two options: to give up and go and cry in a hotel room, or to keep going. All you can do in that moment is to think positively and not think too far ahead. I decided not to quit, and to finish the swim and then take it step by step and somehow finish the race.

I kept going, things changed, and I eventually managed to win the race and achieve a course record. If I had decided to give up, the whole experience would have been over. From one bad moment, with a positive mindset, it went to one of the best days in my career. Looking back, it shows how one negative thought can ruin your day and one positive thought can also save your day.

It's important to always be open to plan C, D, E, F – nothing ever goes according to plan; you need to stay flexible and adjust to the moment. I was not expecting to be stung by a jellyfish. I had to stay calm, accept the situation, and think how to overcome it.

Sometimes, lowering expectation can help. I put a lot of expectations on myself. On that day, I went from my goal of winning the race to just finishing it, and it actually made me feel free. I felt I had nothing to lose as I'd already lost. I was 10 minutes behind after the swim, so I could just go all in.

If something negative happens, it also helps me sometimes to make fun of it. What can happen that's worse than being stung by a jellyfish? Sometimes, shedding some light on a bad moment can help you overcome it.

”

YORK'S NOTES

Being able to reset and refocus quickly is one of the hallmarks of a great athlete, and Daniela is certainly in that category. By being able to manage her negative self-talk and only focus on what she could control in the moment, she refused to allow a pretty major setback to derail her. Daniela quickly reset her approach, refocused, and created a new path which ultimately led her to an unlikely success. Her experience is also a good example of how becoming your own "inner coach" can be so beneficial. At times of high stress, speak to yourself in the way the best coach would, focusing on being motivational, positive, and instructional.

Red Bull
Red Bull
Red Bull
SWISSSIDE
FELT
DT SWISS
DT SWISS
DT SWISS
DT SWISS

YORK'S EXERCISE

AS MATTEO BERRETTINI SAID EARLIER IN THE CHAPTER, ***MAKING SENSE*** OF FAILURE AND ***REFLECTING*** ON IT IN A ***POSITIVE MANNER*** IS ***NOT*** ALWAYS ***EASY.*** BY FOLLOWING THIS SIMPLE FRAMEWORK, THOUGH, WE CAN GIVE OURSELVES THE ***BEST OPPORTUNITY*** TO ***LEARN*** FROM OUR ***LOSSES.***

Firstly, we need to learn the difference between two concepts called dispositional and situational attribution. Dispositional attribution is an internal feeling whereby we make ourselves responsible for the outcome. Situational attribution is where we believe external factors were to blame for a negative result. The next time something didn't go as you'd hoped, try working through these steps. They can be really helpful!

1

To start with, list all the things that actually **went well despite the negative outcome.**

Now, list all the things **that didn't go well,** but were **IN your control.**

Next, list all the things that **didn't go well**, but were **OUT of your control.**

Once you've made your lists, think about which category was **hardest** or **easiest** to find items for.

Finally, **look back** at the things that **didn't go very well,** but were **within your control.** These are the things you can **work on,** and **knowing that** is the **first step** in working out how you can **improve.**

YOUR NOTES

CHAPTER 9

COPING WITH CRISIS

INTRODUCTION

WE ALL HAVE TO FACE A CRISIS FROM TIME TO TIME, WHETHER IT'S IN OUR PERSONAL OR PROFESSIONAL LIVES, WHETHER IT IMPACTS US INDIVIDUALLY, OR AFFECTS THE FAMILY OR OTHER PEOPLE WE LOVE.

IN THIS CHAPTER WE'LL LOOK AT:

Accepting vulnerabilities, seeking help

Dealing with the unexpected

The value of journaling

WE'LL HEAR FROM:

Ben Stokes
"I took steps to open up to people who were very close to me and then I went out and sought help from a professional."

TJ Rogers
"I'm still here doing what I love, and that's all that matters. I'm really thankful that I've had that mentality to just never give up on something you really love doing."

Saya Sakakibara
"I couldn't allow myself to be defeated by the fear. I gave myself another year, but this time decided to do every single thing the way I wanted."

A crisis can come in any shape or size, but always, it seems, at the worst possible time.

It's easy to forget this when we see top athletes perform at such an impossible level, but they are human too, and that means they're as likely to be hit by a crisis as the rest of us.

On top of that, they experience the challenge of their problems often playing out in the public eye, and with the media looking on – from career-threatening injuries to crises of confidence, from health issues to slumps in form.

Whatever the sport, high-performance athletes must become accustomed to coping with a crisis – and, crucially, to face it head on rather than ignore it and hope for the best.

There are lessons that all of us can learn from taking that kind of unflinching approach when the worst happens.

Here are three athletes at the top of their respective sports – cricket, skateboarding and BMX – explaining the obstacles they've faced and how they tackled them.

At the end of the chapter there will be an exercise, focusing on the use of journaling as a powerful processing tool, which should be a useful preparation for facing future challenges.

BEN STOKES

ENGLAND'S TALISMANIC TEST CRICKET CAPTAIN IS ONE OF THE WORLD'S MOST GIFTED ALL-ROUND PLAYERS.

An inspirational captain, Ben has helped transform the way Test cricket is viewed around the world by encouraging his team to play in a fearless style that's brought success and entertainment in equal measure. His ability to influence a match with bat or ball also makes him unmissable when in action out on the field.

But before he took over the mantle of English skipper, he suffered a very public mental health battle, taking time out from the sport to recuperate before returning to the elite level of cricket.

The rebuild hasn't been easy, but he has been very open about the battle in a bid to help not just his teammates but also the wider public who might be facing up to their own similar demons.

"

I was almost putting emotions and feelings into a glass bowl. The glass bowl got too full and exploded. And then everything just got a bit too much for me at that time. Looking back, it was definitely a build-up over a long period of time of almost compressing emotions or feelings and not being comfortable in speaking about them to anybody.

I was by myself in a hotel room where the team was staying. It was very early in the morning. There were things that started happening that had never happened to me before. It's very hard to look back on that specific moment, but what I do know is – and I can openly say – I wasn't very good at talking to people before that fateful day. I'm a lot better now at doing that, and I'm a lot more open about speaking to the right people, who I feel comfortable speaking to about certain things.

It's not just your professional life that it can take hold of, or just your personal life – it's definitely both. Some people feel it affects their personal life before their professional life, whereas for me I felt it was affecting my role in terms of what I had to do as my job, which was obviously go out and play cricket.

As important as the physical side of the sport is, the mental side is huge. You always need to be in the right frame of mind to perform under a huge amount of pressure, especially what you do at the international level.

The steps I took were to open up to people who were very close to me, and then I went out and sought help from a professional. The gentleman I ended up speaking to came highly recommended, so I had a lot of long and good face-to-face chats with him.

He actually gets it; he understands it, so he could explain to me what was going on by listening to the things that I was telling him, because – although it's great to be able to open up to people who are close to you and just for them to listen – it's even better to be able to go and do the same thing with someone who can then explain everything to you so you get an understanding of what's going on.

I felt that I was having to be almost 10 different versions of myself in 10 different situations. Now, I am what I am, and I can just be me. People will love me, people will hate me, but at least I'm confident that I'm giving the best account of myself

> *I WAS ALMOST PUTTING EMOTIONS AND FEELINGS INTO A GLASS BOWL. THE GLASS BOWL GOT TOO FULL AND EXPLODED. LOOKING BACK, IT WAS DEFINITELY A BUILD-UP OVER A LONG PERIOD OF TIME OF ALMOST COMPRESSING EMOTIONS OR FEELINGS AND NOT BEING COMFORTABLE IN SPEAKING ABOUT THEM TO ANYBODY.*

S1, EP 4

LISTEN TO THE PODCAST HERE:

and not trying to live up to anybody's expectations and almost be fake. I've said many a time, I'm on medication daily now, which I'm not afraid to say. Within our team, I've been very keen to make sure that we have performance psychologists and clinical psychologists available to everybody.

So, when I'm away, I know that if I do ever need to go and speak to either of those two, that they're available. It's not just for me; it's for everybody else as well, and it's worked really, really well.

YORK'S NOTES

As captain, leader, and a star player, Ben is under immense pressure to perform in the crunch moments. When it really matters, everybody looks to him for motivation. In this powerful interview, he shows that it's OK to talk about your emotions, your vulnerabilities, and your weaknesses, and doing so in no way diminishes you as a player or a leader. It's inspiring, in fact, and demonstrates that despite his bulletproof exterior, he's human. There's no doubt that his confidence in talking to the right people, has helped him personally, and it sounds like it's made just as big a contribution to the team set-up as a whole. Ben also shows that he's learned to stay true to himself and be completely authentic. He's not living up to the expectations of anyone else. That's true leadership.

Red Bull
adidas
GM

SKATEBOARDING SAVED MY LIFE. I WENT THROUGH CANCER, AND IT WAS THE ONLY THING THAT HELPED ME SURPASS A LOT OF THE NEGATIVITY AND THE THINGS THAT I WAS DWELLING ON.

S2, EP 7

LISTEN TO THE PODCAST HERE:

TJ ROGERS

CANADIAN SKATEBOARDER TJ ROGERS HAS TAKEN THE ROAD LESS TRAVELLED TO GET HIMSELF TO THE FOREFRONT OF THE ELITE SKATEBOARDING SCENE.

Born and raised in Calgary, Canada, TJ had his work cut out to make a name for himself. But he packed up, headed to Los Angeles to turn professional, and forged a stellar career.

His is also a story of triumph over adversity. His parents weren't able to raise him, so he moved into foster care in his formative years, a period of his life he has likened to jail time. But he also recognises it was influential in making him the positive force he has become both in and out of his sport.

His more recent struggle has been a battle with testicular cancer, back in 2022. He credits skateboarding with saving his life and once more giving him purpose after his surgery and a course of chemotherapy.

" —

Skateboarding saved my life. I went through cancer, and it was the only thing that helped me surpass a lot of the negativity and the things that I was dwelling on. It gave me a sense of hope and something where I could give back to other people and tell them, "Hey, everything in the world is crazy right now but it could always be worse, so never get distracted and know your end goal of where you want to be."

I had just turned 30 and recently got a dog. We were playing, and she hit me in my testicle region so hard that it really hurt. I finally went to get it checked out and I got an ultrasound. They called me two hours later saying I needed to go to a specialist immediately as they'd found a nodule on my testicle,

and they didn't know if it was benign or cancer. I had surgery, and they took one out. I could feel the whole inside of my legs and core depleted, but within three weeks I was skating again.

I had to do chemotherapy. That time was probably one of the most challenging things I've had to overcome in my career. Each round of chemo consisted of five days, and I would have to go in for 7am and do a four- to five-hour infusion.

Every time I had a break, I skated through chemo. During those 16 days off after each round, I could see the transformation in myself – losing my hair, losing my eyebrows, losing literally everything on my body.

I'm still here doing what I love, and that's all that matters. I'm really thankful that I've had that mentality to just never give up on something you really love doing. Even as a young kid, I would always have a piece of paper of what tricks I wanted to do and what my goals were.

You always want to have a five-year plan. I never want to be comfortable with my life, because if I am, that's not how I'm truly able to capitalise and live my best life.

I have goals and I have dreams, so I push myself to elevate, to make sure there's no excuses and I can do anything that I want.

YORK'S NOTES

TJ's ability to set long-term goals and stick to them through a crisis is what stands out here. His long-term goals have helped him through challenging times, because he had a reason to fight back. He describes some really challenging obstacles in his life, that for many people would be the end of the dream, but he's shown huge resilience to continue fighting. His story shows that it's not if we encounter the unexpected, but when, and that how we deal with the curveball is the all-important factor. After all, it would be unrealistic to think that if we set ourselves a long-term goal that's going to take a year or two to reach, there will be no obstacles coming our way!

SAYA SAKAKIBARA

THE AUSTRALIAN BMX RACER'S GOLD MEDAL AT THE PARIS OLYMPICS WAS THE CULMINATION OF A THRILLING, AND HIGHLY EMOTIONAL, STORY OF REDEMPTION.

Saya made a choice to follow in the footsteps of her brother Kai when she took up BMX, and as they progressed in the sport it seemed as if the two siblings were destined to compete for the biggest prizes for years to come. But during qualification for the Tokyo Olympics, Kai suffered a terrible crash that left him in a coma for several weeks and put an end to his career. Saya herself went on to qualify, but her dreams of winning the gold medal were dashed when she crashed heavily in the semi-finals. The following year she suffered a series of further accidents, including several concussions, causing her to seriously consider her future in the sport.

This is how she describes the process of dealing with the emotional and physical pain of both her brother's accident and her resulting career journey, and her plans for the future, which include cheering on her brother in his new sport of para-rowing.

" —

My brother Kai is a prominent part of my BMX journey. His love for BMX and riding bikes – I wanted a piece of it as well. I wanted to be the same as him. It was all I ever knew.

He kept a training diary from nine years old. When I then started journaling as a young girl, it was about my training and what I could do better. Now, I use it to process my emotions and as my sounding board. By the end of an entry, I'm writing positive things about the situation. It feels like magic. You don't even think about doing it, but you're solving your own problem. It's a cool tool that I use. It's also a reminder that you have to record and capture things, as life goes by so fast.

In 2020, Kai was in a coma for six weeks after a crash. It was a touch-and-go situation. The doctors did their best, but it was out of their hands whether he was going to wake up, and how he would be if he woke up. There were no answers.

It was a horrific time. For me, I think his injury impacted me at different times. It hit me the most after the 2021 Games because, up until then, I'd had this goal of doing it for both me and Kai. It's what we dreamed of together. I was so motivated to get there, I don't think I had the time to process everything. After that, everything came crashing down and I realised what I had really lost. My best friend, my teammate, my travel buddy.

It made me realise, what is BMX without Kai? I'd been doing it because of him, so if he's not doing it, why am I doing it? My answer was to quit. In 2022, I suffered my fifth concussion, and I really didn't want to go through it again. You have this feeling of not feeling right.

As I started to tell people I was quitting, I just had that nagging feeling of, "You're not done yet. I can't quit now!"

I couldn't allow myself to be defeated by the fear. I gave myself another year, but this time decided to do every single thing the way I wanted. Every decision was for me. As much as I wanted Kai to be there

> EVERYTHING CAME CRASHING DOWN, AND I REALISED WHAT I HAD REALLY LOST: MY BEST FRIEND, MY TEAMMATE, MY TRAVEL BUDDY.

S3, EP 3

LISTEN TO THE PODCAST HERE:

on my journey, he was on a different path; I couldn't keep living the lie that he was with me.

I started making changes, and it was empowering. I was taking back control, and every decision was for me.

Kai is still fully supportive of me, and I get to be there now for his rowing journey. I like to think that we inspire each other. I hope my BMX inspires him to keep going, and he's a living and breathing inspiration for me.

YORK'S NOTES

Saya has had to overcome so much, and her triumph in Paris was one of the most heartwarming of the whole Games. It's interesting how she has used journaling as a processing tool both inside and outside of competition. A competition journal is where you make notes in pre-defined categories that you can track over time. The more you do it, the more you can reflect on each competition and start to learn from it. Journaling can be used in many different ways, though. It can act almost like a mental recovery tool to close certain moments or days and prepare for what's coming next. More and more athletes are doing it, and it's something absolutely everyone can try.

Red Bull
Sqorz
ace

YORK'S EXERCISE

AS WE HEARD EARLIER FROM SAYA, USING ***JOURNALING*** AS A TOOL TO ***PROCESS YOUR EMOTIONS*** CAN FEEL LIKE ***"MAGIC",*** AS IT CAN HELP ***REDUCE STRESS*** AND BRING ***CLARITY*** TO A CHALLENGING SITUATION.

If you do it often enough, it becomes part of your daily routine and almost happens automatically. Many people dismiss journaling without properly trying it, so here are some tips on how to kick-start your diary entries and enjoy the benefits from it.

1

There are **many types** of journaling, so find the one that **suits you best.** Maybe it's putting all your thoughts down on a blank piece of paper, or maybe it's using the prompts in a gratitude journal to help you. **Experiment** and see what works **best.**

2

Consider using a **pen and paper.** This method makes the experience **more private** and because writing is slower than typing, it allows you to **process** your **thoughts** better and choose your words more **carefully.** There are also **fewer distractions** than when using a phone or computers, so you should be more **focused.**

3

Remember that a daily **positive reminder** can increase your **self-confidence** and **self-awareness.** So, whatever form of journaling you do, consider starting your day on a **positive note** by writing down, for example, three things you're **grateful** for that day.

Set a reminder or alarm if you'd like help remembering to journal. There is **no** set time, though, as to how long it should take. For some, it can be **minutes,** and for others, it can be **much longer.**

Try it for at least **four weeks** so you really get to know if it **will work** for you or **not.** Don't dismiss the idea after **one time** of trying. And if you miss a day or two at some point, that's **not** a reason to give up – just **continue** from the day you remember to write again.

YOUR NOTES

CHAPTER 10

DEVELOPING STAYING POWER

INTRODUCTION

TO ACHIEVE ANYTHING IN LIFE, WE NEED TO BE ABLE TO STAY THE COURSE – AND THAT TAKES RESILIENCE, DETERMINATION, AND SELF-BELIEF.

IN THIS CHAPTER WE'LL LOOK AT:

Staying single-minded

Developing resilience

Maintaining motivation

WE'LL HEAR FROM:

Lindsey Vonn
"I think my biggest mental strength is overcoming adversity. I have a really high level of determination – if I set my mind to something, I won't stop until I achieve it."

Mutaz Barshim
"One second, I had just cleared the highest jump in the world, and a few moments later, I was in a wheelchair. I couldn't walk, my season was done, possibly my career was done."

Kate Courtney
"Endurance sports are not just about physically pushing through, but also being able to remain mentally focused, motivated, and positive over the long haul."

Sometimes it might also mean making tough decisions to adjust our goals, or even dealing with the disappointment of letting one dream go in order to make another possible.

Here, it might be useful to bear in mind a fact that most people see for themselves in the transition from school to work: star students do not always go on to become high achievers. In fact, the most successful people tend to be individuals who are not always perfect, but have developed the ability to respond to setbacks, and who work hard to finish what they start.

Just as important to remember is that however committed we are, we all have our off days or times when things just feel too tough – and that's absolutely fine! When we're in those moments, it's important to acknowledge our feelings and show ourselves some understanding. Just because we miss one day's training, it doesn't mean all is lost. Lapses are part of the journey, and finding the determination to keep striving and get back to it will guarantee you steadily build your performance levels over time.

In this chapter we hear from a trio of inspiring athletes about the techniques they've developed to manage the trials of injury, expectation, and constant competition. You'll learn how they cope with the pressure of such demanding training schedules and how they avoid being derailed. And you'll get useful insights that will help you build your resilience to keep going on your chosen path.

LINDSEY VONN

TALENT AND SHEER GRIT HELPED MAKE LINDSEY VONN ONE OF THE MOST SUCCESSFUL SKI RACERS OF ALL TIME – AND THE SAME QUALITIES HAVE NOW FIRED A QUITE INCREDIBLE COMEBACK.

With 82 World Cup wins and Olympic gold and bronze medals to her name, Lindsey is a true sporting great.

But hurtling down a mountain at speeds of up to 85 miles (135km) an hour is a high-risk pursuit, and throughout her career Lindsey came back from many dramatic crashes and painful injuries that might have spelled the end for other less determined athletes. In the last race of her professional career in 2019 – before she launched her remarkable comeback – Lindsey's determination got her back on the mountain and enabled her to win another World Championship medal, despite having suffered a serious crash the week before.

Now she is back writing a new chapter of her story, after partial knee replacement surgery meant she could ski without chronic pain for the first time in years. It's yet one more example of the remarkable resilience of a unique athlete.

"

I think my biggest mental strength is overcoming adversity. I have a really high level of determination – if I set my mind to something, I won't stop until I achieve it.

I'm willing to sacrifice and continue to work long past what everyone else is willing to do in order to achieve my goals. It comes, I think, mainly from my mother. She was the strongest person I knew, and it just wasn't ever a question whether I would work hard or whether I would pick myself back up if I fell; it's just something that's ingrained in me from her. Obviously when you have injuries or adversities, your path to your goal changes. But I always just reset my goals. I figure out: what is it going to take now to get to the top? How long do I have to work to get back to where I want to go?

The most pressure I've ever felt was at the Olympics. I had just injured my shin and I didn't

> THE BEST ADVICE I CAN GIVE IS TO ALWAYS BELIEVE IN YOURSELF. IF YOU DON'T BELIEVE IN YOU, THEN WHO ELSE WILL?

S1, EP 9

LISTEN TO THE PODCAST HERE:

know if I was going to race, and I'd never won an Olympic medal and I was 24 or 25 years old. So I just felt an extreme amount of pressure. But I was able to perform because I thought of all the times that I was disappointed, all the times that I didn't make it, and all the times that I had sacrificed, my family had sacrificed, to get to that point. I mean, I've never skied so hard in my life – I almost went off course four times!

I remember coming to the finish line and seeing my time and just collapsing – I think out of joy, but also out of pure relief that after all the sacrifices my entire life, that I finally was able to achieve that.

My final race, that was my final goodbye, and I was so nervous. I used all of the emotion and all of the pain I was in. I had two braces, I had three fractures in my left leg, I had a bone bruise in my right leg, I felt like I was being held together by duct tape.

I skied with basically only my mind and my heart. I willed myself to the finish line. Mind over matter forced me to the finish line, and I was able to get a medal in my final race.

There are so many things I've learned from ski racing that have helped me in my life now, specifically being able to focus on one thing and being very driven and goal oriented and never giving up.

The best advice I can give is to always believe in yourself. If you don't believe in you, then who else will? Whatever your dreams are, you just have to believe in yourself and work hard. And if you fall, just pick yourself back up and keep going. ”

YORK'S NOTES

Although there's no doubt Lindsey has always been an incredible athlete, what made her such a winner was her attitude. Even in the final race before her (temporary) retirement, when her body was broken, it was her determination that got her back up and over the finish line. Lindsey has what is often called mental robustness – basically, the passion and perseverance to set and meet long-term goals. Because even though talent and luck are important, neither is enough without the mental robustness to help you stay committed to your goal when the going gets tough.

Whatever our goals are, we're certain to encounter some obstacles along the way. So, what Lindsey said about resetting her goals is important – and is similar to what Marc Márquez mentioned in Chapter 7. When setbacks happen, we need to take a moment to recalibrate and calmly ask ourselves, in these changed circumstances what is it going to take to reach my aim? And how long do I have to work to get back to where I want to go – as Lindsey has done with her remarkable comeback!

IF YOU LOVE SOMETHING, DO EVERYTHING YOU CAN TO GO FOR IT. IT MIGHT SEEM IMPOSSIBLE, IT MIGHT FEEL DIFFICULT, BUT IF YOU TRULY BELIEVE IN YOURSELF, IT'S WORTH IT.

S1, EP 11

LISTEN TO THE PODCAST HERE:

MUTAZ BARSHIM

QATAR'S TRACK AND FIELD SUPERSTAR IS A THREE-TIME HIGH JUMP WORLD CHAMPION AND AN OLYMPIC GOLD MEDALLIST.

It was in Tokyo in 2021 that Mutaz provided one of the most memorable stories of the Games, showing great sportsmanship by asking if he and his Italian rival Gianmarco Tamberi could both receive a gold medal after clearing the same height.

But for all the success, he's also had his share of setbacks, and he speaks candidly and thoughtfully about what it takes to keep coming back, no matter what life throws at you.

" —

In 2018, I injured myself really badly and broke both of my ligaments on my take-off leg. I was competing in this track meet in Hungary, and I actually felt good, I felt ready to jump high, but as soon as I started running towards the bar, when I planted my left foot, it just snapped.

One second, I had just cleared the highest jump in the world, and a few moments later, I was in a wheelchair. I couldn't walk. My season was done; possibly my career was done. I saw a doctor who had been operating on sports injuries for 40 years and he said it was the worst injury he'd ever seen. He told me the chances of me coming back were 1 per cent, almost impossible.

Before the surgery, my training was always fun, but coming back, it was a real struggle. And then you start questioning yourself: am I ever going to be able to do what I do again? Am I ever going to be able to jump again? This is my passion; if it just stopped now, who am I going to be? What am I going to do?

But I was hungry to go back, and I found calm and peace within myself. I decided I would

do everything I could, and if it was meant to be, it would be.

I needed to rearrange my thoughts and ask myself, what do I really want? And once I did that, I felt like a different person. From that moment I was willing to take a challenge, and I started working really hard.

First of all, my feet were so stiff, and the ligament was really tight. I could barely move, and I felt like that for a long, long time. Eventually I started getting stronger – but the jumps still weren't clicking. And then I realised I couldn't compare myself to my best; I was a beginner again and I needed to start from almost zero.

One day in training, I did a jump that was so good, it almost felt like a jump from before the injury, and it was the first time ever I felt like I was actually flying. Once I landed, I looked at my coach and my tears started dropping – I couldn't believe it!

And in that moment, I felt like I would never doubt myself again, whatever situation I'm in, even if all the circumstances are against me. That jump I did during that training, I think it was the highest jump I've ever done in my life.

And at that moment, I knew I was back. Imagine if I had decided to give up – I would never have experienced that achievement, I realised then that when I looked back over my life, I didn't want to be in that position. So I would say, if you love something, do everything you can to go for it. It might seem impossible, it might feel difficult, but if you truly believe in yourself, it's really worth it.

"

YORK'S NOTES

Even in the face of a devastating prognosis from his surgeon, Mutaz managed to find the mental, emotional, and behavioural flexibility necessary to defy the odds and kick-start his recovery. We can all learn from the way Mutaz's combination of humility and self-belief sustained him and made the seemingly impossible possible. When we hit a big bump in the road, giving up is often the easier option but, as Mutaz says, it's instructive to consider how you might feel if you let go of your goal. Asking yourself what your goal means to you will help you reconnect with your motivation and that in turn will give you renewed determination.

KATE COURTNEY

KATE GREW UP IN THE MOUNTAIN BIKING MECCA OF MARIN COUNTY IN NORTHERN CALIFORNIA AND HAS GONE ON TO WIN SOME OF THE SPORT'S GREATEST HONOURS.

Cross-country star Kate was one of the co-hosts during the first season of *Mind Set Win*, sharing presenting duties with Cédric Dumont. The 2018 World Champion and 2019 World Cup champion brought first-hand experience of the mental and physical demands of top-level sport.

What gives Kate the mental fortitude to push through pain, fatigue, and adverse conditions is her persistence. She says that forming habits around her training makes it simpler for her to stick to her aims. For any of us struggling to be consistent, her message is straightforward – even if you miss a day, go back the next day and the day after that – just keep showing up and you'll be amazed by the progress you can make!

"

I think my greatest mental strength is persistence. Endurance sports are not just about physically pushing through, but also being able to remain mentally focused, motivated, and positive over the long haul. And obviously there's a lot of sub-skills to that – there's setting adequate goals, having a really good plan to get there, but that persistent mindset of just, day in and day out, being dedicated to what it takes to make those incremental steps, I would say has been my greatest strength in my career.

I've had mantras at a lot of races – just a few words that help me centre into what the goal is, what to think about during the race and to come back to if ever things become challenging. My favourite mantra from last year was "accept and commit".
It was about accepting the uncontrollability, the uncertainty, which was a huge challenge for me during the pandemic, and committing to the moment, winning that little inner battle of, "Will I push the edge? Will I keep going? Will I get the most out of myself in every possible moment, both in training and in racing throughout the season?"

And it was something I came back to, particularly in moments of challenge, where you have to accept getting a flat tyre for example, but committing to a complete effort and to maintaining the type of mindset that will allow you to get the best result possible given the circumstances you have on any given day.

One of the biggest challenges coming out of the Olympics was adjusting my goals and taking a long view of what it would take to get back to the top. If I just said, "I want to win every race the next year", knowing that I had to build back, I think it would have been a pretty discouraging experience.

But instead I was able to sit down with my coaches and make a really good three-year plan. So, for the first year, our goal was consistency and getting back into the top 10. And it set a really stable foundation for when we could aim a bit higher.

That's where, again, that persistent mindset and that ability to just continually evolve and show up and do the work comes in handy and is critical to reaching those goals that often take years and years to build towards as an elite athlete. Yes, motivation

> *MOTIVATION IS PART OF MY JOB, BUT I THINK STRUCTURE AND DEFINING WAYS TO SET YOURSELF UP FOR SUCCESS GOES MUCH, MUCH FARTHER. IF YOU BUILD IN THOSE SYSTEMS, YOU WILL MAKE IT POSSIBLE TO JUST SHOW UP AND GET BETTER AND DO SO CONSISTENTLY.*

S1, EP 6

LISTEN TO THE PODCAST HERE:

is part of my job, but I think structure and defining ways to set yourself up for success go much, much farther.

You only have so much motivation, and if you build in those systems, you will make it possible to just show up and get better and do so consistently. Don't miss more than one day of a habit. And rather than saying, "Oh, now I'm off track", try saying, "It's not happening today, but it's happening tomorrow. This day was an anomaly, but I am still a person who meditates every day." It's about committing back to that habit again and again.

YORK'S NOTES

Kate understands that the road to success can be long, and motivation alone won't get her to where she wants to be. Creating a structure that includes a clear plan, a solid routine and the ability to adjust her aims in response to circumstances is key to helping her persist in her goals. We all know how easy it is to make a resolution, but sticking to it is another matter. If you miss a day at the gym, all isn't lost – show yourself some compassion. The key is to maintain your dedication and make sure you go back the next day and the day after that.

If you're eager to find out more on how to set and achieve your resolutions, head to your go-to podcast platform and listen to our six *Mind Set Win* New Year's Special episodes at the end of season 2.

SHIMANO
13

YORK'S EXERCISE

WHEN WE'RE CONFRONTED BY ***CHALLENGES,*** IT'S ***ESSENTIAL*** TO HAVE ***TECHNIQUES IN PLACE*** TO HELP US ***STICK*** TO OUR ***GOALS.*** KATE COURTNEY MENTIONED HOW SHE USES ***MANTRAS*** TO HELP HER STAY FOCUSED ON HER GOALS. ***"ACCEPT AND COMMIT"*** WAS HER GO-TO MANTRA.

Finding a mantra that's meaningful to you can be very effective when you feel like you're flagging. So, think of a situation where you'll benefit from a mantra – like when you're trying to master a new skill, for example. Decide on your goal and follow these steps to figure out your own personal mantra.

1

Think of what you want to **achieve** or something you want to **improve** at.

2

Brainstorm what you need to **tell yourself** to be able to **succeed.** For example, if you're learning an instrument or trying out for a sports team, your mantra might be, **"I can learn and improve."**

Keep it **short** and **clear.**

Keep it **positive.** Instead of, "I don't want to feel tired", repeat to yourself, "I feel **powerful.** I feel **energised.** I feel **awesome.**"

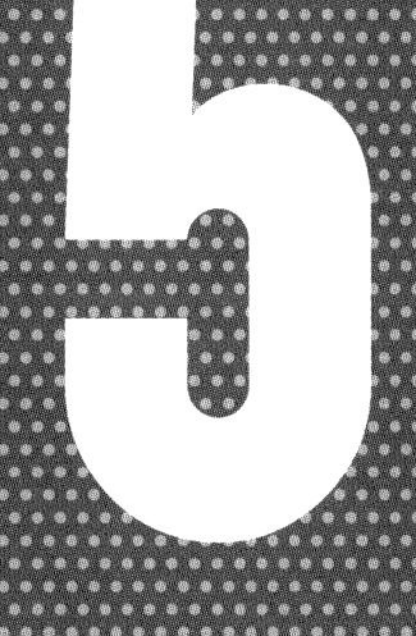

Keep it **actionable.** Use your mantra as a **reminder** of what you're **capable** of, how you want to feel, or what you plan to do. **"I am ready. I am thankful. I can do this."**

Keep it in your **mind.** Use your mantra when you need to **direct** your mind away from negative feelings, thoughts, and actions. Let it **help** you steer your mind towards a **positive attitude.**

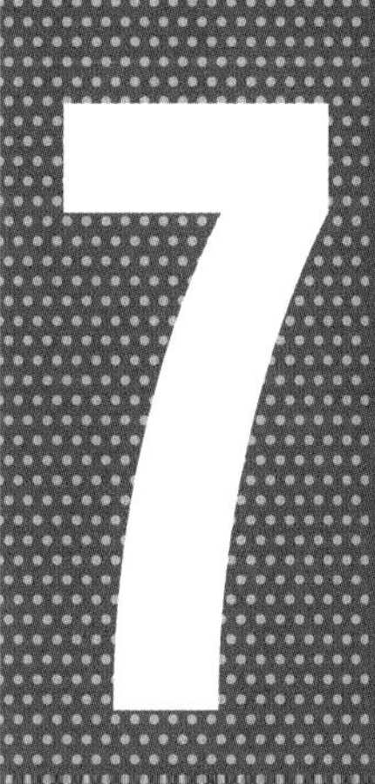

Now take a few moments to write down **your mantra.** Say it out loud a few times – the more you **practise** saying your mantra, the **easier** it will become.

Write it somewhere: on a bracelet, on the inside of a book, or make it your screensaver.

Remember, your mantra can almost be seen as a **contract** with **yourself** – the **guiding principles** you agree to follow whenever you need them. **Framing** your mantra like this can help you **stick** to what you **agreed upon** with yourself.

YOUR NOTES

YOUR NOTES

CHAPTER 11

KEEPING CONTROL

IN THIS CHAPTER WE'LL LOOK AT:

- **Using tactical body language**
- **Practising compartmentalisation**
- **Thriving on pressure**

WE'LL HEAR FROM:

Elena Rybakina
"I think tennis is a game like chess, but active chess. You hit the ball and then you need to know what your opponent is gonna do."

Chris Matthews (aka Lethal Shooter)
"I learned how to use the frustration to get better. So I ask myself, why am I frustrated? What can I do better next time to not get frustrated?"

Marcus Kleveland
"When I'm under pressure, I feel like I always do better. When I really know that I need to land or I have this thing pressuring me, then I'm like, 'OK, now I have to win!'"

INTRODUCTION

BEING IN COMPLETE CONTROL OF A SITUATION IS SUCH A NICE FEELING, BUT IT'S FAIR TO SAY THAT, FOR MOST OF US, LIFE RARELY SEEMS TO RUN THAT SMOOTHLY.

You know how it is – when you must be on time, but the train is late, the clock is ticking, and there just aren't any good options; or when the situation requires your full attention, but the notifications keep coming on your phone, you're struggling to concentrate, and, of course, last night you hardly slept!

The truth is that whatever our goals, we'll never be able to stop life pelting us with distractions or unexpected problems. One of the keys to improving outcomes is in developing effective ways to react to such situations – to channel emotion and find a way to reassert at least some measure of control.

Preparing to handle things going wrong at some stage doesn't mean planning exactly what you're going to do in every eventuality. As we saw in Chapter 7, it can be a good idea to assume that things are not going to go exactly to plan and prepare for how we're going to react when, inevitably, something unexpected happens – perhaps by setting aside emotions (or at least appearing to set them aside) to give ourselves the feeling of being in control.

Finding ways to focus on the job in hand not only frees up headspace for us to pursue our goals, but it can also give us some perspective on our feelings. This can mean that when we return to re-examine those feelings again later on, it's in a more constructive way.

In this chapter we'll hear from three world-class athletes who have risen to the top in highly competitive and scrutinised environments. Let's learn a bit more about how they manage to stay in control even when things are not going to plan.

> NO MATTER WHAT THE SITUATION IS, I TRY TO BE CALM AND NOT SHOW IF I'M UPSET OR I'M ANGRY. I TRY NOT TO SHOW MY EMOTIONS. IT STILL HELPS ME NOW, AND I THINK IT CAN SOMETIMES CONFUSE MY OPPONENTS.

S2, EP 3

LISTEN TO THE PODCAST HERE:

ELENA RYBAKINA

KAZAKH TENNIS PLAYER ELENA RYBAKINA HAS PERFECTED THE ART OF ONLY LETTING HER OPPONENTS SEE EXACTLY WHAT SHE WANTS THEM TO SEE.

Renowned for her poise, precision and powerful serve, Elena took her first Grand Slam title at Wimbledon in 2022 when she upset third seed Ons Jabeur. But at a moment when others might have screamed or punched the air, Elena allowed herself just a little smile before walking calmly to the net.

In a high-pressure sport like tennis, being able to maintain control often gives her the edge over an opponent who can't read her body language. Handling her emotions so well has helped her become the champion she is.

"

I think tennis is a game like chess, but active chess. You hit the ball and then you need to know what your opponent is gonna do. No matter what the situation is, I try to be calm and not show if I'm upset or angry. I try not to show my emotions. And I think this is something that worked especially well in the beginning – when no one knows you and you are calm on the court and then you play really well. Now, it still helps me, and I also think it can sometimes confuse my opponents. I have no idea where my poker face came from, but I think I had it even when I was a kid playing tournaments. Maybe it's my reaction to the stress.

At Wimbledon, when I made it to the final of course, I was very nervous at the beginning of the match. It was my first final and I felt very emotional, even though I was trying to keep a very straight face. Inside there was really a lot going on. And I remember the first set went really badly for me. My serve wasn't working; it was pure emotions.

After I lost the first set, I went to take a toilet break just to breathe a little bit. And I was telling myself that it's just a match, and I believe I'm gonna play another final, so I just need to do what I usually do and forget about what's happening around me. I convinced myself that no matter if I win or lose, I already did a great job, and I should just try to enjoy the experience. Of course, it wasn't easy to enjoy since it was so emotional. But after that I played a much better second set because I was trying to focus on every point, and after winning one game and then a set, it was much easier.

I speak a lot with my coach about it not being good to always stay calm on court. Sometimes I need to show my emotions, especially if I'm not playing well and something is not going as I'd like it to go. In those situations, I need to show my opponent that I'm still there and I'm still fighting. There are moments in the match where you need to really kind of squeeze your opponent.

This is something that we are trying to work on. Maybe other players are too angry on the court or show too many emotions and they need to work to be more calm. But for me, it's kind of the opposite. Tennis is such a quick sport, and I think the faster you can move on from being frustrated or sad, whatever it is, the faster you go back to actually fixing the problem.

"

Red Bull

YORK'S NOTES

Elena uses body language to show her opponent that she's constantly in control. During the match, she might not feel the same way inside, but at least to her opponent, she's showing that she's very calm, very controlled, and dominant in the situation. We're continually communicating via our body as well as with our words, so whether you're at work or even in social situations, it's important to be aware of what you're saying to other people and to yourself through your gestures and your stance. Even if you're someone who needs to vent your emotions, allow yourself to let them out briefly, but then try and regain your positive body posture afterwards. You'll be amazed at the difference it makes.

> *SOME OF THE BEST PEOPLE IN THE WORLD, THEY'RE GREAT AT WHAT THEY DO, BECAUSE WHEN THE BIG MOMENT COMES, THEY'RE ABLE TO BLOCK OUT EVERYTHING. IF YOU WANT TO BE GREAT, YOU CAN'T THINK ABOUT WHAT YOU DID IN THE PAST; YOU'VE GOT TO THINK ABOUT THE PRESENT.*

S1, EP 20

LISTEN TO THE PODCAST HERE:

CHRIS MATTHEWS
(AKA LETHAL SHOOTER)

THE FORMER BASKETBALL PLAYER, ALSO KNOWN AS 'LETHAL SHOOTER', IS RECOGNISED AS ONE OF THE SPORT'S MOST EFFECTIVE AND SOUGHT-AFTER COACHES.

Chris's career as a pro basketball player took him all over the world, but in 2016, he realised just how effective he could be as a shooting coach and made a major career transition that has seen him provide coaching to elite NBA and WNBA players like Dwight Howard, Anthony Davis, Candace Parker, and Skylar Diggins-Smith.

Chris had a difficult journey to glory from an underprivileged childhood in Washington, DC. Along the way, he had to learn how to control his emotions and focus on his game in order to get to where he is today – an admired coach, mentor, and one of the most creative minds in the sport.

“ —

Growing up, my coaches used to pull me out of games when I missed and put my head down. They'd say, “Don't you ever put your head down – you're one of the best shooters in the nation. Get back in there, keep your head up, and keep shooting that basketball!”

I used to get really frustrated when I was young. I remember a club championship game, and I was playing really bad and yelling out loud just to cover it up. And that's when my coach was like, “We don't care if you're missing – just don't be frustrated, because you're going to mess the team up.” And for the second half of that game, I was free. I really wasn't frustrated at my mistakes, and I played great.

I learned how to not bottle up the frustration, because it can blow, but to use the frustration to get better. So I ask myself, why am I frustrated? What can I do better next time to not get frustrated? Because if something negative does happen and you hold on to that, as you're trying to do something positive, they don't match very well. If you want to be great, you need to find what helps you and stay locked in.

There were things that I realised helped me before games, like don't overeat, listen to soothing music, and work on breathing and being calm. Of course, if you're by yourself and you're working out and you need to let it out, scream. But, when you're in that moment, that's not the moment to do it. You'll lose it if you do that.

Some of the best people in the world, they're great at what they do, because when the big moment comes, they're able to block out everything. If you want to be great, you can't think about what you did in the past. You've got to think about the present.

There's certain times in basketball and in life that you have to be calm, but there's certain times that you have to turn that kick on. You can use those things as motivation and a positive influence to get you over the mountain, and that's what I do. I think about certain traumas or certain things I went through in life that helped me to get where I am today.

But, you know, if you're able to bottle up all these things and know what your end goal is and to control your mental state, I think anybody can be successful.

— ”

YORK'S NOTES

The level of self-awareness shown by Chris shines through here. Notice how he becomes acutely aware of how he feels, and how he can use those emotions in the most productive way possible. Whether that means letting them out in his performance or stashing them away to process later, he's able to set aside powerful emotions like frustration to simply focus on his next shot. But as well as learning to push through and perform, critically, he's able to express and process those emotions at the right time so he can truly move forward. What's even more incredible about his process is that in moments of intense pressure, he's able to recall those strong emotions and use them to his advantage. We can all relate to the need to shut out anxiety or even put aside excitement in order to get a job done. If we use this technique of compartmentalisation, it can be an asset to help us manage the inevitable stresses of life while maintaining the ability to perform under pressure.

Wilson
Red Bull

MARCUS KLEVELAND

NORWEGIAN SNOWBOARDER MARCUS KLEVELAND KNOWS ALL ABOUT PERFORMING UNDER PRESSURE – HE'S BEEN DOING IT FOR MORE THAN A DECADE.

Marcus jumped onto the scene as a 13-year-old when he pulled off one of the biggest tricks in professional snowboarding, a triple cork.

He's since gone on to become one of the most inspiring riders in the sport, recognised for his innovation and as a winner of multiple X Games and World Championship medals. But as he says in his interview, learning how to manage the pressure of high-profile competition and to stay focused has been critical to his success.

"

When I'm under pressure, I feel like I always do better. When I really know that I need to land or I have this thing pressuring me, then I'm like, "OK, now I have to win!"

I remember the first couple of contests that I did – I was so nervous, I couldn't really handle anything, and I always ended up in last place. But I feel like the more you do something, the more you get used to it. If you get one podium or do well at one contest, you want to do well at every single contest.

In snowboarding, usually we have three runs and the two best count. So if you mess up on the first run, you're like, "OK, I need to be really focused." You need to really feel like you can do it, go into your mind, and visualise your trick and try to be positive.

If there's a trick I'm trying that's not working out, I go back to another trick. Because if you try a trick more than 10 times, you'll end up losing focus. So you need to go back to another trick and then wait for another opportunity to try again.

But if it's a contest where I don't do well, and I'm bummed, I give myself half an hour to be mad and then after that, I'm like, "OK, stop being mad and get back on the board!" You gotta be harsh on yourself sometimes, but only for a decent amount of time. There are always new chances.

In competitions or training, I always listen to music. It kind of calms my nerves and gets me in the right mindset. Music has always been there, helping me with everything. I hear the music really well when I'm standing up top, ready to drop in. And once I drop in, the music just goes silent. Then once I land, it's like, boom! It's there again.

It's the focus that puts the music away once you ride. I've always listened to music while riding because it's such a helpful thing to do. If it's a bad day, you put on music and then it's a good day. And that's what I feel like music really helps me with.

I just want to try and be in my own mindset, be focused, and drop in, and try and do the best I can do. That's all any of us can do.

"

> IN COMPETITIONS OR TRAINING, I ALWAYS LISTEN TO MUSIC. IT KIND OF CALMS MY NERVES AND GETS ME IN THE RIGHT MINDSET.

S1, EP 8

LISTEN TO THE PODCAST HERE:

YORK'S NOTES

It's good to remember that pressure or stress can actually be very positive. Many athletes will only ever set a personal best or world record in high-pressure situations because they thrive off it. Marcus also uses the energy he gets from high-pressure situations to help him focus. Instead of becoming overwhelmed by the circumstances and losing control, he manages to harness the emotional excitement he experiences to elevate his performance. Finding ways to cope with pressure – really, to thrive on it – is crucial if you want to be the best version of yourself. After all, pressure is something we all experience on a daily basis. I'm sure many of us have felt how much harder it can be trying to reverse park when people are watching!

But if things aren't working out as you'd hoped, one useful tactic Marcus highlighted is to shift your focus, give yourself a break, and come back to the task later on. Take the pressure off yourself if you can, because after all, as Marcus says, there will always be the next chance. And finding ways to shut out distractions can be so helpful before a pressurised situation. For Marcus, music gets him in the zone and keeps him positive, but for all of us it will be different. You might prefer to clear your head by taking a walk or doing some breathing exercises. Whatever it is, finding a mental space where you feel relaxed and positive every time you know you're going to be confronted with pressure will help you remain composed and stay in control.

YORK'S EXERCISE

IF YOU HAVE SOMETHING IMPORTANT YOU NEED TO FOCUS ON, **COMPARTMENTALISATION** CAN BE A USEFUL TOOL.

Say you're about to have an important meeting but you're thinking about that urgent email that's just landed in your inbox or the bad traffic that almost made you late, you could come across as being distracted and uninterested, maybe even a little erratic. Your emotions won't be an asset, and you won't have time to process them before you need to be at your best.

But for some people, the ability to compartmentalise doesn't come naturally. So let's look at a technique to help you refocus in crucial moments.

You know how people always say, push it to one side or file that away? Well, it can be helpful to actually imagine doing that by following these simple three steps.

Take a moment to close your eyes and imagine a **filing cabinet.** What does it look like? Is it green or gun-metal grey? Is it tall, so you're standing in front of it, or is it by your desk, handy for where you're sitting? Either way, it has **three drawers, right?**

Now, think about actually placing the **emotions** you're feeling inside one of the drawers of the filing cabinet – let's say the **top one**. If there's something **tangible** that's got to you – a text or an email someone's sent, perhaps – you can think about putting that inside too, but as long as you're **filing away** the feeling, that's a **good start.**

3

Finally, imagine **closing the drawer.** Really concentrate on the satisfying thud the drawer makes as it closes. Give it one **final push** with your hand – concentrating on that feeling of the metal on your skin – then take a **final beat** and **open your eyes.**

4

This process of imagining filing those **feelings away,** and leaving them for later, can help ensure you are **fully present** as you deal with the situation in **real time.**

But remember, this is **not** a case of **file and forget!** You have to **return** to that filing cabinet once the situation **has passed**, when you're with friends or family, or just feeling **safe** and **comfortable** at home. That's the time to **revisit** those feelings and start **addressing them constructively.**

Q&A

PROFESSOR ADAM NICHOLLS

Adam Nicholls is Professor of Psychology at the University of Hull in England and has spent nearly two decades unlocking secrets to athlete wellbeing and peak performance.

There can't be many psychologists who have conducted more research into how emotional control can enhance athletic performance than Adam.

From his research, he has discovered that it's being able to manage stress levels in high-pressure situations that gives high performers an edge.

Alongside his role at the university, the author of the textbook *Psychology in Sports Coaching* regularly works with athletes and coaches to provide them with the tools to develop their mental strength. As an accomplished Brazilian jiu-jitsu competitor himself, these are techniques that he's refined through his own experience.

So we were fascinated when Adam joined us for an interview to share some of his insights.

Could you talk a little about the importance of mental strength in general?

There are several reasons why mental strength is important. It allows us to manage adversity more effectively, which is linked to resilience. Mentally tough people, I think, also have a better ability to suppress any fear of failure. So they're more focused on what they want to achieve rather than what can go wrong. They're generating what is known as a "challenge state".

When we're in a stressful situation, those who have got the most mental strength are able to draw their attention to the different solutions that can aid their performance and wellbeing. This is known as the "broaden and build" theory of positive emotions. It allows us to build our physical, social, and intellectual resources over time to cope. Doing this allows us to increase our resilience, so by successfully adapting and thriving in difficult situations and learning new strategies to do that, our confidence in our ability to cope increases and then our ability to handle and adapt to future stressful situations improves.

”

MENTALLY TOUGH PEOPLE, I THINK, ALSO HAVE A BETTER ABILITY TO SUPPRESS ANY FEAR OF FAILURE.

So being able to manage stress under pressurised situations is key here?

Definitely. If you can do it, you won't let stress distract you or impact your physical performance. You won't let it impact your decision-making. What I think differentiates between the good, the elite, and the super-elite is their ability to perform under the most intense stress. I think this is vital. If you can't cope with stress, the most intense stress, you can't perform.

In the world we live in, controlling and managing stress in day-to-day life is an essential skill for everyone, right?

Yes, I think it helps with both high performance and high wellbeing. It's essential for anyone. There's evidence to show that the people who get to the top of their professions, or those who can perform at the highest level for a sustained period, are able to deal with the stresses they encounter.

WHEN WE'RE IN A STRESSFUL SITUATION, THOSE WHO HAVE GOT THE MOST MENTAL STRENGTH ARE ABLE TO DRAW THEIR ATTENTION TO THE DIFFERENT SOLUTIONS THAT CAN AID THEIR PERFORMANCE AND WELLBEING.

You mentioned a challenge state – what is this?

There's evidence to show that we have two types of state: a challenge state and a threat state. A challenge state is when we're focusing on what we want to happen and what we want to achieve, whereas a threat state is focusing on what can go wrong. When we generate a challenge state, it impacts us both psychologically and physiologically. It dilates the blood vessels so that more blood can go to the brain and the muscles to aid performance, and it also generates positive emotions.

How do we achieve this state?

Well, there are several ways. So prior to performing, you can identify a specific area of performance that you want to improve on. I'll give an example. For a golfer, it might be improving the number of fairways you hit. In tennis, it might be the percentage of first serves that go in or the average speed of a serve. So it's about improving your own standard of performance, and by focusing and concentrating on that, we're helping to generate this challenge state, because you're setting yourself a self-reference challenge.

Can this be applied to anything? Like being in the office?

Absolutely, in presentations for example. I use these things when I'm presenting, giving lectures, interviews. It's for any situation where there's a performance demand. It just so happens I work in sport and I post on LinkedIn all the time, and everyone's like: "Oh, this could work in business!" And, yeah, it could, and it will.

What are some of the biggest signs of stress that you've seen in your research?

We have a tendency under stress to engage in avoidance behaviour. So when we're really stressed and the competition is hard, there is a tendency for some people to withdraw their efforts. They stop trying to achieve their goal – they may have a goal before competing but when it gets hard, their performance might deteriorate a little bit and then they just give up in some ways. Sometimes, people are not aware of these things, and that's the biggest issue, particularly in young athletes.

Are there any techniques for stopping these negative thoughts?

Everyone has a tendency to allow negative thoughts to creep in sometimes. And when they do, we need to control them. There are several ways we do that.

One, I really like either saying "stop" to yourself, whether out loud or just to yourself, and then replacing that with a thought that is more conducive to performance, that is, what you want to happen, what you want to do.

Another good way is seeking support. Our support networks are crucial. And one thing I really like, which comes from the "goodness of fit" approach, is identifying someone in your support network who's good at providing emotional support and someone who's good at providing informational support. First, you list the names of the people in your support network, such as mum, dad, coach, boyfriend, girlfriend. And if they're really good at providing emotional support, you put an E next to their name. And if they're good at providing informational support, you put an I next to their name. When you have a problem that requires support, you go to the appropriate person for the best support. And there's lots of evidence that this works, and works well.

My final strategy is mindfulness meditation. There's really good evidence that engaging in mindfulness meditation changes the structure of your brain, particularly in the prefrontal cortex, the insula, and the hippocampus. And that allows you to manage emotions more effectively. In essence, it's enhancing mental strength; it's enhancing resilience through regular practice of this meditation.

Out of the strategies that you've outlined, which one would you say works best to manage stress?

One thing that we found in my research is that effectively coping with stress involves the combination of a variety of different strategies. It's not just one – it's using them together. It's about having an effective toolbox and using everything within your toolbox rather than one specific thing.

Do you think that anybody, regardless of their stage in life, personality, or their emotional background, can improve their mental strength?

Absolutely, 100 per cent. What you'll find is that some people will be able to build their mental strength quicker than others, and some will have a higher starting point, but everybody can build their mental strength by taking some simple steps, no matter how old.

IT'S ABOUT HAVING AN EFFECTIVE TOOLBOX AND USING EVERYTHING WITHIN YOUR TOOLBOX RATHER THAN ONE SPECIFIC THING.

What would you say is the first thing someone could do to make such improvements?

I would say the first thing to do is think about the stressful situations in your life, and then identify some that you coped well with and others where you didn't cope effectively. Write those down – write what you did – and already you'll have a list of examples of effective and ineffective coping strategies. That might trigger awareness, because quite often we're not aware. So by just making this list, quite often people will say, "Wow! I didn't think of that!", or "I didn't realise this didn't help", or "When I did this with that, that really helped."

That would be the first step to being able to reflect on what works and what doesn't work, and then building the mental strength up from there.

YOUR NOTES

CHAPTER 12

FINDING PURPOSE

IN THIS CHAPTER WE'LL LOOK AT:

- **Finding your why**
- **Inspiring your community**
- **Connecting with your heart**

WE'LL HEAR FROM:

- **Siya Kolisi**
  "Sometimes your purpose has to be more than just about you. It must mean that, if you don't do this, you must think about how many other people it will affect."

- **Molly Carlson**
  "I rely on my #BraveGang to inspire me, and they rely on me to keep inspiring them through posting my organic content and being real."

- **Carissa Moore**
  "Everyone expects me to keep chasing world titles and being on the Tour, but why is this meaningful to me? I got to a place where I was doing it for the wrong reasons and it really bled into my performances."

INTRODUCTION

PURPOSE IS VITAL BECAUSE IT PROVIDES US WITH A SENSE OF MEANING AND DIRECTION IN OUR LIVES.

A sense of purpose can guide our decisions, influence our behaviour, and, crucially, provide us with motivation, particularly when the going gets tough. Whatever you're hoping to achieve, whether it's a new skill you're mastering or a tricky situation you're tackling, understanding how this aligns with your values, passions, and goals will be a huge help.

Many people find themselves on a particular path not because of a series of conscious, well-thought-out decisions, but just because they were good at something and liked it well enough, or even because it's what someone else wanted them to do. Whether that's true for you – or if you just have the feeling sometimes that you're drifting along – it can be helpful to take some time to ask yourself why you're doing what you do. Having a firm idea of the why behind your actions will provide you with a North Star to guide you on your journey.

As we'll see in the stories in this chapter, a strong sense of purpose can also fire our self-belief so that when we encounter setbacks, we have the energy to keep going. And when we feel our lives have meaning, this enhances our overall sense of wellbeing and fulfilment. Many elite athletes have a story like this – a belief that has formed the foundation for everything they've built to become world class – and it's something we can build too.

What's raised the three athletes you're about to meet above the competition has been keeping sight of their purpose. It's helped them sustain their motivation and achieve remarkable feats. So read on to get inspired and find ways to connect to your own individual purpose.

> *WHEN YOU TALK ABOUT PURPOSE, YOU HAVE TO KNOW WHY YOU'RE DOING SOMETHING, AND YOUR 'WHY' HAS TO BE FAR BIGGER THAN YOUR SELF-DOUBT.*

S2, EP 2

LISTEN TO THE PODCAST HERE:

SIYA KOLISI

THE FIRST BLACK CAPTAIN OF THE SOUTH AFRICAN RUGBY TEAM LED THE SPRINGBOKS TO VICTORY IN 2019'S RUGBY WORLD CUP, THEN MADE HISTORY BY INSPIRING A SECOND CONSECUTIVE WIN IN THE SPORT'S SHOWPIECE TOURNAMENT IN 2023.

On the field, Siya is a dynamic player, with a rare blend of speed and power. From early on in his career his electric performances coupled with his cool professionalism and leadership skills made him stand out from the crowd.

Raised in a poor township by his teenage mum and grandmother, Siya often felt the gnaw of hunger. When he was spotted and offered a rugby scholarship to the prestigious Grey High School, he realised this was his way out of poverty and an opportunity to change the course of his life and the lives of the people he loved.

Since that day Siya has always had a clear purpose, which underpins his drive to be the best in rugby – to be a beacon of hope for kids like him from the townships.

Here's Siya talking about his background, and the importance of the Kolisi Foundation, which works to tackle inequality in South Africa.

“ —

Rugby was big. I loved it when I was young. Then I got opportunities along the way, as people saw me play and they gave me a chance. A teacher just believed in me and took me to trials, and I made it to a school. And then when I actually got a bursary, I said, "I'm going to use this; this is going to be what's gonna change my life and my family's life." And it did.

I come from a tough background, and in South Africa there are so many others who come from the same background as me. I wake up every day and I carry myself, in a way, remembering that I must push every single time because others are looking at me and I want to be that little bit of hope for them. I'm working as hard as I can so that the kids can see it's possible. No matter how tough your background is, you can still make it.

When we won the Rugby World Cup in 2019, there were xenophobic attacks in South Africa. People were fighting. So we went to the World Cup knowing all of that was happening, and we wanted people to be proud and to be happy for that moment. We played for South Africa because we knew if we won, the rest of the country would win too.

Playing wasn't pressure; it was more of a privilege because you're doing what you love, and you know it can change how people feel back at home – that's the kind of drive and mindset we have. In the team, we had different races and different languages, different backgrounds. We showed what you can do when people from different places have one common goal. Rugby has done so much in our country; it was used by Mr Mandela, to help bring people together. So all of those things we think about before we play in battle.

When you talk about purpose and vision, you have to know why you're doing something, and your "why" has to be bigger than the doubt you have over yourself. Sometimes your purpose has to be more than just about you. It must mean that, if you don't do this, you must think about how many other people it will affect.

It's not just about me; it's about my family. I provide for my family and my extended family too. I have a foundation and there are kids that we look after. When I do well and I play well, people want to work with you; people want to be associated with you and they want to donate to what you're doing. So I know the harder I play, the more I get up in the mornings even when I don't want to get up, I know kids are getting fed.

And that's my "why"; that's what I want to do – make the world a better place by working in my foundation.

"

YORK'S NOTES

Siya knows exactly why he gets up every morning to train hard and improve himself as an athlete. He wants to give back to his country and to people around him – and that provides him with a strong purpose. We won't all have the same purpose, of course. Some people, like Siya, will have a community-based passion that drives them, while others may be motivated by a desire to innovate, to change the world, or to share what they have learned with those around them. Taking the time to discover your own personal "why" is important because it can guide you when you're uncertain and give you that extra motivation to keep on when you may be tempted to take it easy, or even give up.

MOLLY CARLSON

CANADIAN HIGH DIVER MOLLY CARLSON IS A REGULAR ON THE PODIUM AT RED BULL CLIFF DIVING, AND A PASSIONATE ADVOCATE FOR MENTAL HEALTH.

Molly's talent was instantly obvious when she finished second on her debut in the competition in 2021, and she's gone on to finish runner-up in the World Series in 2022, 2023 and 2024 – second only to Rhiannan Iffland.

Molly has talked quite openly about her experiences of debilitating anxiety that led to body dysmorphia and an eating disorder before she joined the World Series.

The learnings from this "dark" period of her life, though, have gone on to inspire millions of people around the world, which has in turn provided Molly with a new sense of direction and purpose.

Like many others, Molly started posting creative content on TikTok during the pandemic and built up more than one million followers in just one week using the hashtag #BraveGang. By speaking openly about her fears, experiences, and anxieties, Molly doesn't just dive for herself any more, but for her entire #BraveGang community.

Here's how, through inspiring others, Molly has found true fulfilment and become one of the best high divers in the world.

"

After posting, I started reading the comments, and they were all, "This girl is so brave!" and "I want to be like her!"

I just saw bravery everywhere and I kept thinking, if a million people follow me, how can I give back to them? I came up with the idea to create my own hashtag #BraveGang. Everyone can use it to share their own brave stories. We all have one – not everyone's jumping off a cliff, but everyone has their own brave journey.

It was crazy how many people were using this hashtag. I was so inspired every single day. I wanted to keep it going, so I continued to share my journey so people would never feel alone and could share their journeys as well.

It wasn't just the positives, but for the dark times too. The Brave Gang helped me out during the anxious times, and my community is commenting to help each other through difficult times as well.

It was magical to see this community form through a simple hashtag. I rely on them to inspire me, and they rely on me to keep posting my organic content and keep being real. I love that I have a community who will call me out. It humbles me and reminds me of who I should be. It's amazing.

The community not only inspires me on a daily basis, but every time I'm up on the platform and I'm nervous. It's the little things like this that get you out of the dark headspace and bring me back into a happy time. In my mind, I know that I'm going to do this dive not just for me, but for everyone that's a part of my journey.

I sometimes think, how did I get to this point? From a small girl from Ontario to representing Canada and doing the world's hardest dive, and it's all thanks to this community, really.

> IN MY MIND, I KNOW THAT I'M GOING TO DO THIS DIVE NOT JUST FOR ME, BUT FOR EVERYONE THAT'S A PART OF MY JOURNEY.

S1, EP 22

LISTEN TO THE PODCAST HERE:

I think a lot of people see me as a cliff diver, but it's so cool to have more than just cliff diving and being known for more than just your sport. A lot of people come to my channels for comfort, and to be that person for other people. Being a mental advocate is something I'm so proud of.

I never want another teenage girl to go through what I did, alone.

”

YORK'S NOTES

Molly's story shows us that a sense of purpose can materialise when you least expect it. When she posted her first video on TikTok, she never expected the huge online community she would create. Now, she uses social media to hugely positive effect. By choosing to be so honest and authentic, Molly has become an inspirational figure to her online community. Sharing her experiences, both good and bad, to help others gives her the added purpose and mental strength to overcome her fears and perform to the best of her ability. Research shows us that providing acts of kindness and choosing to help people can actually improve our own mental wellbeing by producing endorphins. Molly and her #BraveGang demonstrate this in the best possible way.

Red Bull

> *THE THREE CORE PILLARS ARE TO LIVE FEARLESSLY, LEAD WITH LOVE, AND BE AUTHENTIC. AND THOSE ARE THINGS THAT I'VE PICKED UP ON MY OWN JOURNEY THAT HAVE HELPED ME LIVE A MORE POSITIVE, JOYFUL LIFE OF PURPOSE.*

UNCUT, EP 13

LISTEN TO THE PODCAST HERE:

CARISSA MOORE

SURFING LEGEND CARISSA MOORE IS A FIVE-TIME WORLD CHAMPION. SHE WAS THE FIRST WOMAN TO WIN OLYMPIC GOLD IN SURFING DURING THE SPORT'S DEBUT ON THE BIGGEST STAGE IN 2021 AT THE TOKYO GAMES.

At just 21 she was inducted into the Surfers' Hall of Fame, and the State of Hawaii declared January 4 to be Carissa Moore Day.

But even a career as glittering as Carissa's has its challenges. After a tough season struggling to find motivation and meaning, Carissa started her foundation, Moore Aloha, in 2018 to help girls and women build self-awareness and community.

And it is these goals that are giving Carissa purpose as she prepares to step away from the Championship Tour.

" —

We all have different timings on our journey; we're all here for a unique and individual special purpose. I started a charitable foundation called Moore Aloha, and I talk a lot about what the foundation is built from and the values I try to share with the girls and young women that are a part of our events and programmes.

And the three core pillars are to live fearlessly, lead with love, and be authentic. And those are things I've picked up on my own journey that have helped me live a more positive, joyful life of purpose. I just feel, when I'm more connected to being me and what feels right to me, everything is so much better. And by being me, I can be more joyful with other people and share more love with other people.

There's definitely points in my life when I've disconnected with my heart and found myself really in my head. But I want to be completely honest – it's an ongoing challenge to get out of the head and stay in the heart. So that's when I have to reel it back and I have to call in my sports psychologist and start journaling again and take some quiet moments to go for a hike and be with nature or go for a surf.

There was a period of three years when I felt disconnected. That was one of the biggest low points, after I won my third world title; I was lost and asking myself, "Why am I doing this? Everyone expects me to keep chasing world titles and being on the Tour, but why is this meaningful to me?" I got to a place where I was doing it for the wrong reasons and it really bled into my performances. My results were the worst they had ever been, and my relationships were suffering as well.

I thought, "OK, we've got to strip this all away. Let's start from the ground up. And just simplify and start doing those things that bring me joy again."

I've been thinking about this more recently, especially with starting my foundation. What message do I want to share with young women and girls and anyone that is navigating life? I guess it would be centred around being kind to yourself. One of the hardest exercises for me is to look in the mirror and say, "Riss, you did this great today. I'm proud of you." And I think by being kinder and giving ourselves more grace, we're able to give that same grace and kindness to other people. As soon as I start leaning into feeling good and the faith and the love, that's been a game changer for me. — "

YORK'S NOTES

For some people, winning titles or being the best in your discipline can be their entire motivation. But it's interesting that Carissa says it was at a point in her career after winning her third world title that she felt she had lost her way. Instead of just carrying on, Carissa had the courage to stop and re-evaluate. By going back to basics and asking herself some tough questions, Carissa found fresh motivation to move forward positively into the next phase of her career. Surfing the wave of success is thrilling but checking in regularly to question whether your aims are still in line with your values will make sure you stay on course.

YORK'S EXERCISE

WE'VE READ HOW ***CONNECTING*** WITH A ***PURPOSE*** CAN HELP ***INCREASE*** OUR MOTIVATION LEVELS AND ***PUSH*** US TO ACHIEVE ***REMARKABLE FEATS.***

So how can we all find our own "why" in life – that all-important spark that drives us on a daily basis to overcome challenges and reach our peak performance level in whatever we do? Here's an exercise to try at home.

1

Before you close your eyes at night, **pause** and write down three things you were **grateful** for that day.

They might start off being really **big things** like family, careers, and friends, but they can also be **smaller things** like the time you spent doing a hobby.

It's important to take a bit of time to **reflect** on what areas of life are important to you. **Ask yourself** the question, what is it that makes it **meaningful?** Look at your list and think, if one of these things was taken away for a whole month, which would be the **most significant loss?**

4

After a few days, start looking for any **connections** between the things you have written down. Are there some that are all **related** to the same **theme, person, or activity?**

Continue with the process **daily;** by doing so, you'll start to find **key connections** that shape a **larger purpose** and help you find **deeper enjoyment** and **motivation** in the things that are **important to you.**

Q&A PHIL WIZARD

Philip Kim, better known as b-boy Phil Wizard, has become a master at finding his flow when the pressure is really on. With the world watching, the Canadian became the first ever b-boy to win an Olympic gold in Paris with his creative and original style that impressed the judges.

Viewers watching the spectacle will have learned that a competitive breaking battle is not only a punishing combination of sport and art, but an intense mental confrontation as well.

In this revealing interview, Phil talks about how he approaches the challenge of displaying all the attributes required by a top-class athlete – including confidence, adaptability, calmness, and risk-taking – while staying true to himself and his own vision of this unique discipline.

Can you talk about the role of mentality in high-level competition?

I think, when you're competing at a high level in any sport or athletic endeavour, mind games are half the battle. Your mentality is half the battle. When you compete at the top, everyone's physically there, everyone is at the top of their game. It really becomes about who is mentally stronger than everyone else. I've had situations where I wasn't at my best, but I've won some of my biggest competitions because my mentality was in the right state – I was super-focused.

How important is it for you to have people you know around you?

When I compete, I like having my people with me. It plays into my mentality. When you have your boys, the people you love, and the people who make you feel comfortable, you feel a lot more at ease entering a high-stress environment. Everyone has different strategies, and that's something that helps me. Having your friends around just helps calm you down a lot more.

What's the difference between a mentor and a coach, in your view?

In my head, a coach is someone who's just telling you what to do – you have to drill this, you have to do that. For me, a mentor is more like someone you respect, someone you've known for a long time, and someone you feel very comfortable around. It's also outside of just your sport. A mentor is someone you look to for mentality, life advice, whatever it may be. You build that trust. We lean more towards mentorship within the realm of breaking because, yes, we're in the world of sport now, but for us, as an art, it was a culture first.

I THINK THE MOST IMPORTANT THING – AT LEAST I GREW UP LEARNING THIS – IS TRYING TO STAY TRUE TO YOUR ART.

How do you handle feedback?

Everyone has an ego. So, if it's someone that I don't respect and they're giving me feedback, in my head, honestly, I'm like, "Why are you talking?" But if it's coming from someone that you know has your best interests in mind, someone you have a good relationship with, you can put that ego aside and understand, OK, they're just looking at it from an outside perspective. It is important to take that outside perspective and recognise that this person is trying to help you and give you a different opinion.

It must be hard to not take the views of other people personally?

Yes, especially because you hold it so closely. It's not just about sport for us, it's not about who's the fastest and who's the strongest. You're judging our art, and this is our self-expression. So, when people say, "This doesn't look good", or "You shouldn't do it like this", you feel a bit attacked.

EVERY EXPERIENCE, EVERYTHING YOU LIKE, YOU INCORPORATE INTO YOUR DANCE.

How do you stay true to yourself while still remaining competitive?

Competition has been rooted in breaking for the longest time. Even though it's an art, it's a judged art. So, you have to recognise that whenever you go into any competition, you're in the hands of the judges. At least for me, I try not to think about it too much. To be completely honest, I don't really care. I just go and do my thing. If I win, I win. If I lose, I lose. I think the most important thing – at least I grew up learning this – is trying to stay true to your art.

How do you develop your own style in breaking?

It's just living life. As a person, you grow up, find the things you like and dislike, and your experience helps you to recognise those things. It's the same when you're approaching dance. You listen to music and dance to music that moves you. A lot of people, I think, dance to the music they think they're going to hear in competition and practise to that, because they think, "I'll hear this in competition, so I want to be prepared." But the way to develop your own style is to dance to music you like, because that will authentically bring out the movement you want to express. Every experience, everything you like, you incorporate into your dance. For me, I watched a lot of anime growing up, so sometimes I envision myself as an anime character while practising, and that brings out a different side of me that's genuine, because it's something I grew up with and liked. I don't think you ever arrive at a definitive style. The beauty of it is that it evolves as you evolve as a human being. As you grow older, your style will change.

How do you handle the mental challenge of watching your opponent during a battle?

Breaking is hard mentally because you're watching the opponent as you battle. It can really psych you out. If someone does a really good round, you have to be really mentally strong and able, in that moment, to think, "No, I can one-up this person." But it's scary when you see someone right in front of you doing incredible stuff. You could break in that moment, but you're forced to watch it. You can't close your eyes; you have to watch what they're doing. You really have to be ready on the spot and have the right amount of focus, excitement, and adrenaline in your body. You might have something in mind that you prepared in advance, that you now know won't win, so you must stay adaptable.

How do you stay relaxed and focused before a competition?

I have to approach everything in a relaxed manner. If I take it too seriously, I tend to crumble. My technique is to be relaxed, just to have fun with it, and to remind myself that I won't let one day define me. I won't let one competition define me. I'm in this for the long run. I come back to why I started doing this – I love dancing. So I'm in the back, goofing off. I'm talking to my friends. I'm just having fun. I'm joking around, pretending to do their moves, whatever the case is.

How do you replicate the freedom of training in a competition setting?

As simple as it sounds, you're trying to be free in an environment where you're caged. You're in a controlled environment, on stage. Freedom, for me, is when you're training. You're free because there's no pressure to dance. You can dance when you want, take as many breaks as you want, whatever. There aren't a lot of eyes watching. It's a lot more free. Replicating that on a competition stage, where there are judges and an audience, is difficult, but that's the goal. To do that, you must be mentally relaxed, at ease, and comfortable.

There's a lot of risk involved in your performance; how do you approach this?

It's about taking that chance and taking that risk in the moment. It's a split-second decision of, "I can do this", because you're adapting to the music at hand too. So, in the moment, I could take the risk or not take the risk. It's your choice. I could go the safer route or try something, knowing it might not work out. Eventually, as you keep practising and getting better, I think there's probably a biological thing, of your body getting more comfortable, of knowing when you can start taking those risks and you're able to execute more and more. And then, when you get to bigger stages, you're more comfortable doing it, but you must take that step every single time.

IT'S A BALANCE. YOU MUST STAY FOCUSED BUT ALSO BE OPEN TO THE ENERGY AROUND YOU.

How do you adapt your style to different competition environments?

The environment plays a huge role in your style. When you're just in your studio practising or training, it's one thing. But when you're at a big venue, with lights on you and a lot of people watching, it's different. I found that whenever I entered a competition too focused or too stressed, it never worked out for me. I had to remind myself, "I'm here to have fun, to enjoy myself." That's when I performed the best. I also realised that the more I embraced the environment, like taking in the crowd's energy and not shutting it out, the better I danced. It's a balance. You must stay focused but also be open to the energy around you.

A CONTINUOUS PROCESS

We hope you've not only been surprised, uplifted, and entertained by the stories and thoughts of these remarkable people, but that you've also found something in each chapter that resonates with you personally.

This book was never intended to be just about the guests on *Mind Set Win,* but about you, the readers, and your own journey towards a winning mindset.

After coming this far, we'd encourage you to reflect on one more learning – that you should view this journey as continuing rather than something that comes to an end as you finish the final pages.

The athletes and high performers we've met along the way understand that developing mental strength is a continuous process. So even if you've made it all the way through from cover to cover, we hope you'll continue to dip in and out, to try the exercises again, and perhaps refine them yourself.

And look out for special episodes of *Mind Set Win* wherever you get your podcasts, as we continue to introduce you to more great guests, with more invaluable insights, and more ideas on how to build your mental strength.

Your Mind Set Win team

Red Bull

IMPRINT

1st Printing © 2025 Benevento
by Benevento Publishing Salzburg – Vienna, a brand
of Red Bull Media House GmbH, Wals near Salzburg

Owner, publisher and editor
Red Bull Media House GmbH
Oberst-Lepperdinger-Straße 11–15
5071 Wals near Salzburg, Österreich
info@at.redbullmediahouse.com

Design by
Fargo Circle Studio

Typefaces
Bigger
Neue Haas Grotesk
Garamond Premier Pro

Picture Credits
Cover: Red Bull Content Pool: James Mitchell (Lucy Charles-Barclay), Cody Pickens (Lindsey Vonn), Sam Todd (Max Verstappen), Craig Kolesky (Siya Kolisi), Trevor Moran (Jamie O'Brien), Sebas Romero (Marc Márquez), Domenic Mosqueira (Carissa Moore), Adam Klingeteg (Mondo Duplantis)
Inside: Red Bull Content Pool: p. 3: Adam Klingeteg, 5: Ryan Miller, 6: Craig Kolesky, 10: Niko Zuparic, 12: Niko Zuparic, 14: James Mitchell, 14: Julien Blanc, 14, 16: Pat Nolan, 17: Domenic Mosqueira, 18: Zak Noyle, 19: Ryan Miller, 21: Patrik Lundin, 22, 23: James Mitchell, 24: Dom Daher, 26: Xabi Barreneche, 27: Fred Pompermayer, 32: Joerg Mitter / Alinghi Red Bull Racing, 32: Elias Gammelgard, 34, 36: Devin L'Amoreaux, 39: Jonathan Ferreira, 40: Elias Gammelgard, 41: Jonathan Ferreira, 42, 44: Gines Diaz, 45: Daniel Tengs, 52: Tomislav Moze, 52: Graeme Murray, 52: Alex Wood, 54: Graeme Murray, 55: Tyler Ravelle, 56: Graeme Murray, 57: Paris Gore, 59, 60: Gabriele Seghizzi, 61: Samo Vidic, 62, 64, 65: Alex Wood, 70: Kin Marcin, 70, 72: Romina Amato, 74: Ricardo Nascimento, 75: Dean Treml, 76, 77, 78, 79: Kin Marcin, 88: Alfred Jürgen Westermeyer, 88: Will Cornelius, 88: Mark Thompson/Getty Images, 92: Clive Rose/Getty Images, 93: Mark Thompson/Getty Images, 94, 96, 97: Sandro Baebler/The Red Bulletin, 98: Clive Mason/Getty Images, 99: Julian Kroehl, 100: Mark Thompson/Getty Images, 101: Rudy Carezzevoli/Getty Images, 108: Markus Berger, 108: Charlie Lindsay, 108: Marcelo Maragni, 110, 111, 112, 113: Charlie Lindsay, 114: Mathis Dumas, 115, 116: Jordan Manoukian, 116: Jordan Manoukian, 118: Markus Berger, 120: Daniel Hug, 121: Markus Berger, 124: Nuri Yılmazer, 126: Samo Vidic, 130: Daniel Tengs, 133: Florian Eisele/Motivio, 138: Adam Klingeteg, 138: Gold & Goose, 138: Gary Go, 141, 142, 143: Adam Klingeteg, 144, 145, 147: Gold & Goose, 148: Nejc Ferjan, 149: Gary Go, 150: Leo Rosas, 151: Nejc Ferjan, 156: Patrik Fluck, 156, 158, 159: Gabriele Seghizzi, 160: Alexander Papis, 161: Gabriele Seghizzi, 162: Henner Thies, 166, 168, 169: Patrik Fluck, 174: Brett Hemmings, 174: Peter Jamison, 174, 177, 178, 179: Greg Coleman, 180: Allison Seto, 181: Cole Giordano, 182: Anthony Acosta, 183: Dan Mathieu, 185, 187: Brett Hemmings, 186: Andy Green, 192: Gabriele Facciotti, 192: Emily Tidwell, 192: Adam Klingeteg, 194: Gabriele Facciotti, 195, 196: Sebastian Marko, 197: Gabriele Facciotti, 198, 201: Adam Klingeteg, 199: Diaa Amer, 200: Akl Yazbeck, 203: Emily Tidwell, 204, 205: Bartek Wolinski, 210: Koury Angelo, 210, 212, 214, 215: Mihai Stetcu, 210: Daniel Tengs, 216: Cassy Athena, 218: Markus Berger, 219: Koury Angelo, 221: Daniel Tengs, 222: Peter Morning, 223: Syo van Vliet, 230: Craig Kolesky, 230: Zak Noyle, 230: Dean Treml, 232, 234, 235: Craig Kolesky, 237: Romina Amato, 238, 239: Dean Treml, 240: Zak Noyle, 242: Steven Lippman/The Red Bulletin, 243: Ryan Miller, 246: Markus Berger, 249: Dean Treml, 251: Adam Klingeteg
Other: 32, 37: Simon Hofmann - UEFA/UEFA via Getty Images; 70, 80: Alexander Scheuber/Getty Images for MatchMaker; 82: Mark Metcalfe/Getty Images; 83: Clive Brunskill/Getty Images; 91: Mark Thompson/Getty Images; 128: Ross MacDonald/SNS Group via Getty Images; 146: Eric Alonso/DPPI; 156 (Mario Gómez), 163: Emmanuele Ciancaglini/Ciancaphoto Studio/Getty Images; 164: Stefan Matzke - sampics/Corbis via Getty Images; 165: Gerald Matzka/Getty Images

Printed by Neografia, Slovakia
ISBN 978-3-96704-188-0